Fail Harder

"The Power of Taking Big Risks"

Jacob Jones

Fail Harder: The Power of Taking Big Risks
Copyright © 2025 by Jacob Jones
All rights reserved.

Jacob Jones

This book is a work of non-fiction. While the author has made every effort to ensure the accuracy and completeness of the information contained in this book, the author assumes no responsibility for errors, omissions, or inconsistencies. The stories and examples included in this book are based on real-life events, research, and public knowledge and are used for illustrative purposes only.

ISBN: 978-1-300-69490-8
First Edition

Printed in Canada
Lulu Press, Inc.

Dedication
To those who embrace the risk of falling—and the courage to rise again.

Table of Contents:

the biggest missteps hold valuable lessons.

Acknowledgments

Writing a book about failure is ironic in itself because it's impossible to do without stumbling along the way. This project would not exist without the people who inspired, supported, and guided me through its many drafts, setbacks, and breakthroughs. To all of you—thank you for being part of this journey.

To the countless individuals whose stories fill these pages: your courage to fail, learn, and keep going has shaped not just this book, but the way I see the world. Sharing your triumphs and struggles with honesty has been a gift to readers everywhere.

To the mentors and friends who taught me that failure is not something to fear but something to embrace: your wisdom has been invaluable. Thank you for showing me the lessons that come from stumbling and for reminding me to always get back up.

To the readers who pick up this book: your willingness to explore failure as a pathway to growth is an act of bravery in itself. Thank you for giving these words your time, and for choosing to embrace the hard, messy, and beautiful process of learning from mistakes.

Finally, to the people in my life who remind me daily that failure is never final: you are my constant reminder that the best things come not from avoiding failure but from daring greatly. Thank you for cheering me on, even when the road wasn't easy.

This book is for you—for all of us learning to fail harder and rise stronger.

Introduction:

Why Failure is Your Greatest Ally

Failure sucks. Let's not sugarcoat it. It's awkward, it's painful, and it has a nasty habit of showing up when you least expect it—like a party crasher who drinks all your beer and leaves you to clean up the mess. It's the job you didn't get, the business idea that flopped, the relationship that unraveled. Failure is a universal experience, yet it's the one thing we're all trying to avoid. And that's exactly the problem.

We've been conditioned to fear failure like it's the plague. From the moment we're old enough to understand the concept of winning and losing, we're taught that success is good and failure is bad. Work harder, do better, avoid mistakes at all costs. It's the mantra of every classroom, every office, every Instagram post captioned with #hustle. But here's the thing: this mindset isn't just wrong—it's dangerous. It's holding you back.

If you dig a little deeper, you'll find that failure isn't the villain we've made it out to be. In fact, failure is the ultimate teacher. It's the mentor who calls you out on your BS, the coach who pushes you to the edge of your limits, the friend who tells you the hard truth you don't want to hear but desperately need. Failure strips away pretense and ego, forcing you to confront your weaknesses, rethink your strategies, and grow in ways success never could.

This book isn't here to romanticize failure. I'm not about to tell you that failing is fun (it's not), or that you should aim for it (you shouldn't). What I will tell you is that failure is inevitable, and learning to handle it is the most important skill you'll ever develop. Whether you're an entrepreneur trying to build the next big thing, a student figuring out what's next, or someone just trying to make it through the chaos of life, failure is going to happen. The question isn't *if*—it's *when.* And more importantly, it's *what you do next.*

Let's get something straight: this isn't a self-help book that promises a shortcut to success. There are no secret formulas here, no "one weird trick" to avoid failure forever. What you'll find instead are real stories, practical lessons, and the uncomfortable truths no one likes to talk about. You'll meet people who've failed spectacularly and come back stronger, companies that have hit rock bottom and risen from the ashes, and even a few billionaires who've blown it all and lived to tell the tale. Along the way, you'll learn how to embrace failure, use it as fuel, and, most importantly, keep going.

This book is also for the people who feel stuck. Maybe you're afraid to take a risk because failure seems too big, too scary, too permanent. Maybe you've already failed, and you're struggling to find a way forward. Wherever you are, this book is your guide to rethinking failure and redefining success. It's about turning the setbacks into setups and the losses into lessons. It's about failing harder so you can come back stronger.

By the end of this book, you'll see failure for what it really is: not a dead end, but a detour. Not a verdict, but an opportunity. Not the opposite of success, but a crucial part of the journey. Failure isn't here to stop you—it's here to shape you.

So, are you ready to stop fearing failure and start using it? Good. Let's get to work.

Chapter 1:

Welcome to the Fail Club (Spoiler: You're Already a Member)

Failure. The word tastes bitter before it even leaves your tongue, doesn't it? For most people, it's a taboo topic, whispered about like an embarrassing secret or a regrettable late-night text. But here's the truth no one likes to admit: you've already failed. More than once. And guess what? You're going to fail again.

If that sounds harsh, good. Harsh is where growth starts. Let's not sugarcoat it. Life doesn't care about your plans, your five-year goals, or that vision board gathering dust on your bedroom wall. Life is a chaotic, relentless beast, and sometimes it sucker-punches you just for fun. But here's the kicker: failure isn't the enemy. It's the initiation fee for greatness.

Take a moment to think about the most successful people you admire. Steve Jobs was fired from his own company. Oprah was told she wasn't fit for television. Michael Jordan was cut from his high school basketball team. If you're rolling your eyes because you've heard these examples before, that's fine. But consider this: their success stories didn't begin with triumph. They began with rejection, embarrassment, and a deep, soul-crushing realization that they weren't good enough—yet.

Failure is universal. According to a 2019 study by the Association for Psychological Science, people who fail repeatedly are 22% more likely to succeed in the long run compared to those who play it safe. Why? Because failure is a brutal but effective teacher. It strips away your ego, forces you to face your flaws, and—if you're paying attention—teaches you the skills you need to move forward.

In 2016, Sara Blakely, founder of Spanx and one of the youngest self-made billionaires in the world, shared a story about her childhood. At dinner, her father would ask her and her brother, "What did you fail at today?" If they didn't have an answer, he'd be disappointed. The lesson? Failure wasn't just tolerated; it was celebrated. It meant they were trying, taking risks, pushing themselves beyond their comfort zones.

"Failure isn't a verdict; it's the initiation fee for greatness."

That's the problem with most of us. We're terrified of failure, so we avoid it at all costs. We stay in jobs we hate because we're afraid to start over. We keep ideas locked in our heads because the thought of rejection is too much to bear. We settle for mediocrity because the risk of failure seems worse than the pain of regret.

But let me ask you this: what's the worst thing that's ever happened to you because you failed? Did the world end? Did you lose everything? Probably not. The fear of failure is almost always worse than the reality. A 2021 survey by the American Psychological Association found that 60% of people avoid taking risks in their careers due to fear of failure, yet 78% of those same people reported that their worst failures taught them critical lessons they wouldn't trade for anything.

Failure has a way of exposing the truth. It shines a spotlight on your weaknesses, your blind spots, and the lies you've been telling yourself. It's like ripping off a Band-Aid: painful, yes, but necessary. Think of failure as a magnifying glass. It forces you to look closer, to examine what went wrong, and to figure out how to do better next time.

"Success is not final, failure is not fatal: it is the courage to continue that counts."

— Winston Churchill

Take Thomas Edison, for example. When asked about his countless failed attempts to create the lightbulb, he famously said, "I have not failed. I've just found 10,000 ways that won't work." That's the kind of resilience failure demands. It's not about ignoring the pain or pretending it didn't happen; it's about reframing it.

The next time you fail—and you will—don't run from it. Lean in. Ask yourself: What is this trying to teach me? What did I learn about myself, my approach, or my priorities? Failure isn't the end of the road; it's a detour, a recalibration, a chance to pivot.

And yes, it sucks. There's no sugarcoating that. Failure hurts because it's personal. It challenges your identity, your worth, your dreams. But pain has a purpose. According to neuroscientists, failure activates the brain's anterior cingulate cortex, the region responsible for emotional regulation and problem-solving. In other words, failing literally makes you smarter—if you let it.

So, here's your first homework assignment: fail harder. Seriously. Take a risk this week that has a 50/50 chance of blowing up in your face. Ask out that person who's way out of your league. Pitch that wild idea to your boss. Start that side hustle you've been daydreaming about. Whatever it is, go for it. The worst-case scenario? You fail. But now you'll know something you didn't before.

You're already a member of the Fail Club. The question is, are you going to waste your membership, or are you going to use it to level up? Because the secret to success isn't avoiding failure; it's failing with purpose, failing with grit, and failing until you get it right.

Congratulations—you're one step closer to greatness. And it all starts with screwing up.

Chapter 2:

The Comfort Zone: Where Dreams Go to Die

Imagine this: You're sitting in a warm, cozy bubble. Everything is predictable, nothing is scary, and you've mastered the art of staying exactly where you are. It's not a bad life. You're not miserable. But here's the thing—comfort is a slow killer, a subtle thief of ambition, and the sworn enemy of progress.

Let's start with a simple fact: humans are hardwired to seek comfort. Our brains are biologically programmed to avoid risk because, for most of human history, risk meant death. Sabretooth tigers, poisonous berries, the threat of exile from the tribe—our ancestors weren't debating career changes or startup pitches. They were trying not to die.

But here's the catch: in today's world, most of the "risks" we avoid aren't life-threatening. They're uncomfortable. Awkward. Embarrassing. Yet our brains still treat them like that lurking tiger. According to a 2020 study published in *Frontiers in Psychology*, the same neural pathways that lit up when ancient humans faced physical danger are triggered today when we anticipate failure, rejection, or uncertainty.

This explains why the comfort zone feels so good. It's safe. It's predictable. But it's also a trap. Think of it like this: the comfort zone is a beautiful, air-conditioned prison. The longer you stay there, the harder it is to leave. And the saddest part? Most people don't even realize they're locked in.

Take a look at your life. What parts of it feel easy? What routines do you cling to, not because they're fulfilling, but because they're familiar? Maybe it's a job that pays the bills but leaves you uninspired. Maybe it's a relationship that's comfortable but stagnant. Or maybe it's the endless cycle of "I'll do it tomorrow," even though you know tomorrow rarely comes.

Here's a brutal truth: nothing grows in the comfort zone. Growth demands discomfort. It's messy, unpredictable, and often painful. But it's also necessary. A 2021 report by McKinsey & Company found that individuals who regularly stepped outside their comfort zones—whether by taking on new challenges or embracing uncertainty—were 45% more likely to report personal and professional growth than those who stuck to the status quo.

"Comfort feels safe, but it's a trap that keeps you small."

Real growth looks like falling flat on your face during your first public speech. It looks like launching a business that flops or moving to a new city where you don't know a single soul. It looks like fumbling, failing, and feeling out of your depth. And it feels awful—at first.

But here's the paradox: the discomfort you fear is the exact thing that will set you free. The comfort zone isn't just where dreams go to die; it's where they're buried, mourned, and forgotten.

Consider this: in 2015, a group of psychologists conducted an experiment on the concept of "optimal anxiety." They discovered that people performed best—not when they were completely relaxed, but when they were slightly out of their comfort zones. Too much stress leads to paralysis, but just enough discomfort creates focus, creativity, and resilience.

Think about athletes. No one becomes an Olympian by doing the same workout every day. They push harder, lift heavier, and train longer because they know that growth requires pain. The same principle applies to your life. You can't become a better version of yourself if you're unwilling to leave the version you are now behind.

But let's be real—it's terrifying to step into the unknown. That fear you feel? It's your brain trying to protect you, to keep you safe. But safety is overrated. Safety doesn't write bestselling novels or start billion-dollar companies. Safety doesn't solve problems or change the world.

Take Elon Musk, for example. Love him or hate him, the man is no stranger to risk. In 2008, he poured his last $40 million into Tesla and SpaceX, knowing that if they failed, he'd lose everything. Spoiler alert: they didn't fail. But even if they had, Musk wouldn't have regretted the risk. Why? Because staying comfortable—sticking to the "safe" path—was never an option for him.

The same applies to you. Maybe your dreams don't involve rockets or electric cars, but they matter just as much. Whether you want to write a book, start a business, or run a marathon, the process is the same: you have to get uncomfortable.

So how do you start? By taking one small, uncomfortable step. Say yes to something you'd normally avoid. Volunteer for a project you're not fully qualified for. Introduce yourself to someone who intimidates you. These moments of discomfort might feel insignificant, but they compound over time.

> *"A ship in harbor is safe, but that is not what ships are built for."*
>
> *— John A. Shedd*

And when you fail—and you will fail—remind yourself that failure isn't fatal. In fact, it's proof that you're moving in the right direction. The comfort zone will always be there, waiting to lure you back. But every step you take away from it is a step toward the life you're capable of living.

It's not easy. It's not glamorous. But it's worth it. Because outside the comfort zone is where the magic happens. It's where you find purpose, passion, and potential. So stop waiting for the "right time" or the "perfect plan." Stop settling for safety.

The comfort zone is calling. Don't answer.

Failure Vs. Growth

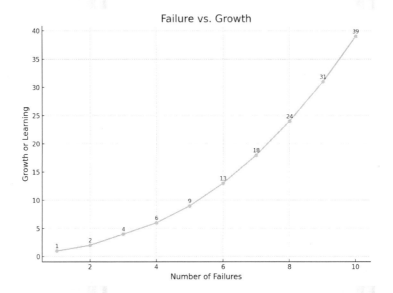

This chart illustrates the direct relationship between failure and growth. As the number of failures increases, so does the level of personal and professional development. Each failure represents a lesson learned, a skill refined, or a new perspective gained, proving that growth thrives on the courage to try, fail, and try again.

Chapter 3:

Fail Fast, Fail Loud, Fail Proud

Failure is a lot like ripping off a Band-Aid. It's inevitable, it stings, and most people prefer to do it quietly in the corner, hoping no one notices. But here's the thing: failing fast, failing loudly, and failing proudly might just be your secret weapon for success.

Let's break that down. First, failing fast isn't about rushing into bad decisions or acting recklessly. It's about taking calculated risks, experimenting quickly, and embracing the lessons as soon as they present themselves. The faster you fail, the faster you learn.

This isn't just motivational fluff—it's backed by science. In 2019, researchers at Northwestern University studied the success trajectories of entrepreneurs and found that those who failed early in their ventures were significantly more likely to succeed later. Why? Because they gained critical insights that allowed them to pivot, improve, and adapt.

Take the tech industry, for example. Silicon Valley thrives on failure. "Fail fast" is practically their mantra. Startups launch with half-baked ideas, knowing full well that most won't make it past the first year. In fact, 90% of startups fail. Yet those same entrepreneurs keep showing up, often launching multiple companies before finding success. Twitter, Instagram, and Slack all started as failed projects. But instead of giving up, their founders used failure as a stepping stone.

So, what does failing fast look like for you? Maybe it's pitching your idea to a mentor before you've fully fleshed it out. Maybe it's testing a new skill, like public speaking or coding, even if you're bad at it initially. The goal isn't to perfect the process—it's to learn what doesn't work as quickly as possible so you can refine your approach.

Now, let's talk about failing loud. This is where most people get stuck. Failure is embarrassing. It's vulnerable. But keeping it quiet only robs you of the opportunity to grow. Failing loudly means owning your mistakes, sharing your journey, and being transparent about the lessons you've learned.

> *"The faster you fail, the faster you learn—and the faster you succeed."*

Think of Sara Blakely, the founder of Spanx. She openly shares the story of her first big failure—bombing the LSAT not once but twice, crushing her dream of becoming a lawyer. Instead of hiding it, she turned her failure into a defining moment, eventually leading her to build a billion-dollar empire. By sharing her story, she connected with others, inspired millions, and proved that failure isn't something to be ashamed of.

In 2017, Harvard Business Review published a study on "intelligent failure," which emphasized the importance of creating a culture where failure is openly discussed and analyzed. Companies that encouraged employees to talk about their failures were not only more innovative but also significantly more profitable. Why? Because transparency breeds trust, and trust breeds growth.

So, how do you fail loudly without sounding like a broken record of self-pity? Start by reframing your narrative. Instead of saying, "I failed at X," say, "I learned from X." Share the process, not just the outcome. Talk about what you did wrong, but also what you're doing differently now.

Finally, let's address failing proud. This might sound counterintuitive—after all, who's proud of falling flat on their face? But failing proudly isn't about celebrating the failure itself; it's about celebrating the courage it took to try in the first place.

In 2004, J.K. Rowling gave a now-famous commencement speech at Harvard, where she described hitting rock bottom before the success of *Harry Potter*. She called failure a "stripping away of the inessential," a period where she discovered her true resilience and clarity of purpose. She didn't shy away from her failures—she embraced them as a badge of honor.

Here's the deal: when you fail proudly, you give others permission to do the same. You create a ripple effect, showing that failure isn't a death sentence—it's a rite of passage.

It's easy to feel defeated when things don't go as planned. But every failure is a deposit in your experience bank. The more you fail, the richer you become—in knowledge, perspective, and grit. According to Angela Duckworth, author of *Grit: The Power of Passion and Perseverance,* grit is one of the strongest predictors of success, and it's forged in the fires of failure.

> *"I've missed more than 9,000 shots in my career. I've lost almost 300 games. Twenty-six times, I've been trusted to take the game-winning shot and missed. I've failed over and over and over again in my life. And that is why I succeed."*
>
> *— Michael Jordan*

If you're waiting for the perfect time to act, let me save you the trouble: there's no such thing. The perfect time doesn't exist, and perfection itself is a myth. What does exist is the willingness to show up, mess up, and try again.

Fail fast. Fail loud. Fail proud. These aren't just words—they're a framework for living boldly. They're a reminder that the only true failure is refusing to try at all. So go ahead, take that leap, and if you fall, make sure everyone hears about it. Because failing isn't the end of the story—it's the plot twist that makes the story worth telling.

Chapter 4:

How to Stop Overthinking and Start Doing

Overthinking is like quicksand for ambition. You take one cautious step, and suddenly you're sinking in an endless loop of "what-ifs" and "maybes." It's the internal monologue that whispers, *What if I fail?* and shouts, *What if I'm not good enough?*

If this sounds familiar, congratulations—you're human. Overthinking is a natural byproduct of an overactive brain, but it's also one of the biggest barriers to success. According to a study published in *Behavior Research and Therapy*, overthinking, or "rumination," is strongly linked to procrastination, anxiety, and even depression. It's a feedback loop of doom: the more you think, the less you act; the less you act, the worse you feel; the worse you feel, the more you think.

"Overthinking is fear in disguise; action is its only cure."

Here's the hard truth: success isn't reserved for the smartest or most talented people. It's reserved for the ones who *act*. It's not about waiting for the perfect moment—it's about taking imperfect action and figuring it out as you go.

Take Jeff Bezos, for example. In the early days of Amazon, Bezos famously told his team to make decisions with "70% of the information they needed."

Waiting for 90% or more, he argued, meant they were moving too slowly. And while not every decision paid off, the act of moving quickly and decisively gave Amazon the edge it needed to dominate the market.

So, how do you stop overthinking and start doing?

Step One: Understand Your Fear

Overthinking is rooted in fear: fear of failure, fear of judgment, fear of the unknown. Your brain wants to protect you, so it conjures up worst-case scenarios to keep you safe. But most of these fears are irrational. A study from *Psychological Science* found that 85% of what we worry about never actually happens.

Let that sink in. The vast majority of your fears are nothing more than mental ghosts. Recognizing this is the first step to breaking free.

Step Two: Set Micro-Goals

Big dreams are intimidating. They're supposed to be. But trying to tackle them all at once is like trying to eat an elephant in one bite. The solution? Break them down into micro-goals.

Want to start a business? Your first step isn't launching a product—it's researching the market. Want to write a book? Start with one sentence. Progress, no matter how small, is still progress. And every small win builds momentum, silencing that overthinking voice in your head.

In 2019, *Harvard Business Review* published research on the "progress principle," which found that making consistent, incremental progress is one of the most significant motivators for achievement. The trick is to start small, then let those small victories snowball.

Step Three: Embrace the Mess

Overthinkers are often perfectionists in disguise. They don't want to start something unless they're certain it will succeed. But perfection is a mirage—it's unattainable and exhausting to chase.

Consider Thomas Edison's approach to inventing the lightbulb. He didn't see his thousands of failed attempts as failures; he saw them as data points. Each one brought him closer to the solution. Success isn't about getting it right the first time—it's about learning from your mistakes and iterating until you do.

Step Four: Commit to a Time Limit

Overthinking thrives on open-ended deadlines. The more time you give yourself to decide, the more time your brain has to overanalyze. Combat this by setting a strict time limit for decisions and actions.

For example, if you're debating whether to send an important email, give yourself 10 minutes to draft it and hit "send." No rereading it 15 times, no tweaking every sentence. Just send it. This sense of urgency forces you out of analysis paralysis and into action.

Step Five: Take Action Before You're Ready

If you wait until you're 100% ready, you'll be waiting forever. Confidence doesn't come before action—it comes *from* action. Studies have shown that taking even small steps toward a goal can significantly increase self-efficacy, or the belief in your ability to succeed.

Think of it like this: action is the antidote to overthinking. The moment you take a step—any step—you break the cycle of rumination and start building momentum.

> *"The way to get started is to quit talking and begin doing."*
>
> *— Walt Disney*

Real-World Example: The Wright Brothers

The Wright brothers didn't overthink their way into inventing the airplane. They didn't have formal engineering degrees or endless resources. What they had was a relentless willingness to experiment, fail, and try again.

In 1903, their first flight lasted 12 seconds. By today's standards, it was a failure. But they didn't see it that way. Every crash, every redesign, every adjustment brought them closer to success. And because they *acted* instead of overthinking, they achieved what many experts of their time thought was impossible.

Your Turn

Overthinking is a habit, and like any habit, it can be broken. The next time you catch yourself spiraling into analysis paralysis, ask yourself this: What's the smallest action I can take right now? Then do it.

Yes, it might be messy. Yes, you might fail. But action—even imperfect action—is always better than inaction. You can't steer a parked car, and you can't achieve anything by sitting still.

So stop waiting. Stop analyzing every angle. Take the leap, make the move, and trust yourself to figure it out along the way. Because the only thing worse than failing is never trying at all.

Chapter 5:

The Risk Recipe: Chaos, Courage, and Coffee

Taking risks is like baking a cake without a recipe. You mix ingredients you think might work, throw it in the oven, and hope it doesn't come out tasting like cardboard. But here's the catch: just like baking, there *is* a method to risk-taking. It's not pure chaos, but a calculated blend of courage, uncertainty, and yes, a little caffeine-fueled determination.

Let's be clear—risks aren't reckless leaps into the void. They're strategic bets on yourself, your ideas, or your potential. But that doesn't mean they're easy. Risks are uncomfortable, scary, and often chaotic. The key is learning how to manage the chaos, summon the courage, and fuel the process with enough energy to keep going.

Chaos: The Essential Ingredient

Risk inherently involves chaos. If it didn't, it wouldn't be a risk. And while chaos feels like something to avoid, it's actually where the magic happens. Chaos is the birthplace of innovation. It's what forces you to adapt, think creatively, and push beyond your limits.

Take Elon Musk, for example. Love him or hate him, the man thrives on chaos. In 2008, Tesla was on the verge of bankruptcy, SpaceX was struggling to get a rocket off the ground, and Musk had poured his entire fortune into keeping both companies afloat. By all accounts, it was a disaster. But in the chaos, Musk made bold decisions, pivoted strategies, and ultimately turned both ventures into massive successes.

The lesson? Chaos isn't the enemy. It's the catalyst. A 2020 study in the *Journal of Business Venturing* found that entrepreneurs who embrace uncertainty and chaos are 60% more likely to succeed than those who seek stability. The key is not eliminating chaos but learning to navigate it.

How do you do that? By shifting your mindset. Instead of seeing chaos as a problem, see it as an opportunity. Ask yourself: *What can I learn from this? How can I adapt?* The ability to stay calm and focused amidst the storm is what separates those who succeed from those who fold.

"Great risks aren't reckless—they're just bold enough to scare you into action."

Courage: The Fuel for Action

If chaos is the setting, courage is the engine. Courage isn't the absence of fear—it's acting despite it. And let's be honest: taking risks is terrifying. The fear of failure, judgment, or loss is enough to paralyze anyone.

But here's the thing about courage: it's a muscle. The more you use it, the stronger it gets. In 2018, researchers at the University of Sydney conducted a study on risk-taking behavior and found that individuals who regularly pushed themselves outside their comfort zones were more likely to take calculated risks in the future. Courage isn't something you're born with—it's something you build.

Start small. Take micro-risks. Speak up in a meeting. Share an idea you've been sitting on. Every small act of courage compounds over time, building the confidence you need for bigger risks. And when the fear inevitably creeps in, remind yourself that fear is just a signal you're doing something meaningful.

Look at the story of Malala Yousafzai. At just 15 years old, she stood up to the Taliban for her right to an education, risking her life in the process. Her courage sparked a global movement for girls' education and earned her a Nobel Peace Prize. Most of us won't face risks of that magnitude, but the principle remains: courage is the driving force behind any meaningful change.

Coffee: The Unsung Hero

Okay, maybe not coffee specifically, but energy. Taking risks requires stamina—mental, emotional, and physical. You can't leap into the unknown if you're running on empty. That's why maintaining your energy levels is a crucial part of the risk-taking process.

Think of it like this: your brain is a battery, and every decision you make drains it. A 2021 study in *Nature Communications* found that decision fatigue—when your mental energy is depleted from overthinking or stress—can significantly impair risk assessment. Translation? If you're exhausted, you're more likely to play it safe.

The solution? Prioritize self-care. Get enough sleep, eat well, exercise, and, yes, indulge in that coffee (or tea, if that's your thing). Risk-taking isn't just about mental toughness—it's about physical resilience, too.

"You miss 100% of the shots you don't take."

— Wayne Gretzky

The Perfect Blend

When you combine chaos, courage, and energy, you get the perfect recipe for risk-taking. But like any recipe, it's about balance. Too much chaos without courage leads to panic. Too much courage without energy leads to burnout. And too much energy without direction leads to wasted effort.

Consider Airbnb. In 2008, the founders were broke, their idea was failing, and the chaos of the financial crisis was in full swing. But instead of folding, they doubled down. They embraced the chaos, summoned the courage to keep pitching their idea, and fueled themselves with pure grit (and probably a lot of coffee). Today, Airbnb is worth billions.

Your Risk Recipe

Now it's your turn. Think about the risks you've been avoiding. Maybe it's starting that side hustle, applying for a job you're not "qualified" for, or finally having that tough conversation. Whatever it is, apply the recipe:

1. **Embrace the chaos.** Don't wait for the perfect moment—it doesn't exist.
2. **Summon the courage.** Start small, but start.
3. **Fuel your energy.** Take care of yourself so you can take care of your dreams.

Risk is messy, uncomfortable, and often chaotic. But it's also the gateway to growth. So, mix your ingredients, take a deep breath, and dive in. The only thing standing between you and the life you want is the risk you're too afraid to take.

The Risk-Reward Spectrum

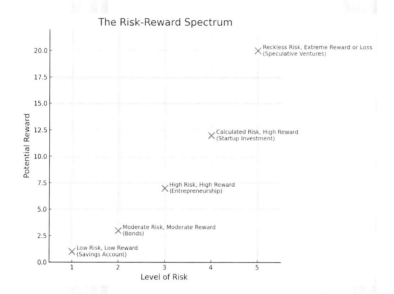

This chart highlights the relationship between the level of risk and potential reward. Low risks yield modest returns, while higher risks offer greater opportunities—but also greater stakes. The key is finding the sweet spot where calculated risks align with achievable rewards, driving meaningful progress.

Chapter 6:

The Failure Spectrum: From Oops to Oh No

Failure isn't a one-size-fits-all experience. It comes in a variety of shapes, sizes, and flavors, ranging from the mildly inconvenient to the truly catastrophic. On one end of the spectrum, there's the harmless "oops"—like sending an email to the wrong person or tripping over your own feet in front of a crowd. Embarrassing? Sure. But life goes on.

On the other end, you've got the full-blown "oh no" failures—the kind that shake your core, drain your bank account, or leave you questioning every decision you've ever made. Losing your job, watching a business collapse, or realizing you've hurt someone you care about. These aren't just moments you shrug off; they're the moments that stay with you, demanding to be unpacked and understood.

But here's the truth: no matter where a failure falls on the spectrum, its value lies in what you take away from it. Whether it's a minor misstep or a massive disaster, failure is a mirror, reflecting who you are and who you're capable of becoming.

Take the story of Blockbuster, for example. In 2000, Reed Hastings, the co-founder of a fledgling DVD rental company called Netflix, approached Blockbuster with a proposal to collaborate. The idea? Blockbuster would promote Netflix in its stores, and Netflix would handle Blockbuster's online presence. Blockbuster laughed him out of the room. They saw no value in a streaming future, clinging to their brick-and-mortar empire. By

2010, Blockbuster was bankrupt, while Netflix was on its way to becoming a global entertainment juggernaut.

Was Blockbuster's failure an "oops" or an "oh no"? At first, it might have seemed like a small mistake—one bad decision among many. But as the years went on, it became clear that this wasn't just a misstep; it was the fatal blow that sealed their fate.

"Every failure falls somewhere between a speed bump and a cliff—you decide how to navigate it."

The lesson here isn't just about bad decisions—it's about the willingness to learn from them. Netflix, in contrast, embraced failure as part of their process. In 2011, the company launched a separate DVD rental service called Qwikster. It flopped so hard that Netflix quickly abandoned the idea. But instead of doubling down on a mistake, they pivoted, returning their focus to streaming and original content. That willingness to adapt turned them into the entertainment giant they are today.

Failure, big or small, carries a similar message: adapt or stagnate. A 2018 study published in *Psychological Science* found that people who reframed their failures as opportunities for growth were 32% more likely to succeed in subsequent challenges than those who viewed failure as a personal shortcoming. The takeaway? It's not the size of the failure that matters; it's how you respond to it.

Consider the infamous Fyre Festival debacle. Marketed as a luxury music festival in the Bahamas, complete with private villas and gourmet meals, Fyre Festival turned out to be a nightmare. Attendees were greeted with FEMA tents instead of villas and sad cheese sandwiches instead of gourmet cuisine. The festival's founder, Billy McFarland, ended up in prison for fraud, and Fyre Festival became a punchline for years.

It's easy to laugh at the sheer scale of the disaster, but there's a deeper lesson in the rubble. Fyre Festival wasn't just a logistical failure—it was a failure of accountability, transparency, and planning. McFarland and his team ignored every warning sign, prioritizing hype over substance. The result was a catastrophic "oh no" failure that could have been avoided with a little more humility and a lot more honesty.

On a smaller scale, think about the failures in your own life. Maybe it was a project at work that didn't deliver the results you hoped for. Maybe it was a relationship that fell apart because you didn't show up the way you needed to. These moments might not make headlines, but they're no less important. Every failure is a chance to reflect, recalibrate, and do better next time.

Thomas Edison famously said, "I have not failed. I've just found 10,000 ways that won't work." That mindset isn't just reserved for inventors and entrepreneurs—it's a framework for life. Every failure, whether it's an "oops" or an "oh no," adds to your arsenal of experience. It's data, feedback, and proof that you're trying.

Even the world of sports is riddled with failure-turned-success stories. Michael Jordan, widely regarded as one of the greatest basketball players of all time, was cut from his high school varsity team. He didn't quit. Instead, he worked harder, using the sting of that failure to fuel his ambition. Years later, Jordan would say, "I've missed more than 9,000 shots in my career. I've lost almost 300 games. Twenty-six times, I've been trusted to take the game-winning shot and missed. I've failed over and over and over again in my life. And that is why I succeed."

"Failure is simply the opportunity to begin again, this time more intelligently."

— Henry Ford

Failure is a spectrum, and every point on that spectrum serves a purpose. The small failures keep you humble. The big failures build your resilience. The catastrophic failures force you to reevaluate everything, stripping away what doesn't matter and leaving you with a clearer sense of what does.

So, where are you on the spectrum right now? Maybe you're recovering from an "oops," or maybe you're still reeling from an "oh no." Either way, the road forward is the same: reflect, learn, and keep moving. Failure isn't the end of the story—it's the plot twist that makes the story worth telling.

And here's the best part: the spectrum isn't linear. Just because you've hit rock bottom doesn't mean you're stuck there. Just because you're riding high doesn't mean you're immune to falling. Life is fluid, unpredictable, and constantly shifting. But no matter where you land, the question remains: what will you do with the lessons failure has handed you?

Because in the end, failure is only fatal if you let it be. The choice is yours.

Chapter 7:

The Science of Screwing Up (And Why It's Good for You)

Failure has been getting a bad rap for centuries. It's been branded as a sign of weakness, incompetence, or even moral deficiency. From our earliest days, we're conditioned to avoid it like the plague. Don't color outside the lines. Don't mess up your homework. Don't miss the shot. Success is the goal, and failure is its evil twin.

But what if I told you that failure isn't just inevitable—it's necessary? That screwing up, falling short, and outright face-planting are some of the most valuable things you can do for yourself? Sound ridiculous? That's probably because you've been taught to see failure the wrong way.

Here's the truth: failure is a feature, not a bug. It's a core component of how humans learn, grow, and achieve greatness. And there's hard science to back that up.

In 2016, researchers at the University of Chicago conducted a study on how people learn from failure versus success. They found something surprising: failure taught people more effectively than success. When participants failed, they were forced to pay closer attention, reflect on what went wrong, and adapt their approach. Success, on the other hand, often bred complacency. People who succeeded were less likely to question their methods, assuming they'd cracked the code when in reality, they might have just been lucky.

Think about it. When everything goes smoothly, how much do you actually learn? Sure, it feels good, but it doesn't challenge you. Failure, on the other hand, forces you to confront your limits. It demands introspection. It makes you uncomfortable—and discomfort is where growth happens.

Take the story of James Dyson, the inventor behind the Dyson vacuum cleaner. Today, Dyson is a billionaire and his name is synonymous with innovation. But his journey was paved with failure. Dyson went through 5,126 prototypes before he created the first successful bagless vacuum cleaner. Five thousand one hundred and twenty-six times he screwed up. Most people would have quit somewhere around prototype 100—or earlier. But Dyson saw failure as part of the process, not a reason to stop. His persistence paid off, and now his company is worth billions.

"Failure rewires your brain to learn faster, think clearer, and adapt better."

Failure isn't just about grit and determination, though. There's a biological component, too. Neuroscientists have found that the brain physically rewires itself after failure. It's called neuroplasticity—the brain's ability to adapt and form new connections based on experience.

When you fail, your brain analyzes the mistake, adjusts its approach, and strengthens the neural pathways that lead to improvement. In other words, every failure makes you smarter.

But here's the catch: failure only works if you let it. If you avoid it, deny it, or wallow in it, you're missing the point. To benefit from failure, you have to own it. You have to look it in the eye and say, "Okay, what's next?"

That's where a lot of people get stuck. Failure feels personal. It stings. It's easier to blame someone else, make excuses, or retreat into self-pity. But those reactions are counterproductive. A 2018 study published in *Personality and Social Psychology Bulletin* found that people who took responsibility for their failures were significantly more likely to achieve success later on. Why? Because taking ownership empowers you to change.

Think about the Apollo 13 mission. In 1970, NASA faced one of its greatest failures when an oxygen tank exploded on the spacecraft, threatening the lives of three astronauts. Instead of panicking or pointing fingers, the NASA team got to work. They analyzed the failure, improvised solutions, and ultimately brought the astronauts home safely. That mission, despite its setbacks, is now remembered as one of NASA's finest moments—a testament to what can happen when failure is met with accountability and resilience.

The same principle applies to everyday life. Whether you're dealing with a failed exam, a business venture gone wrong, or a personal relationship that's fallen apart, the first step is to own it. Acknowledge what happened. Accept your role in it. Then ask yourself: What can I learn from this?

Here's where it gets tricky: learning from failure doesn't mean dwelling on it. There's a fine line between reflection and rumination. Reflection is productive. It's about extracting lessons and moving forward. Rumination is destructive. It's replaying the failure over and over, beating yourself up, and staying stuck.

"The greatest teacher, failure is."

— Yoda (Star Wars)

A practical way to avoid rumination is to reframe your thinking. Instead of asking, "Why did this happen to me?" ask, "What is this teaching me?" It might sound like a small shift, but it's powerful. It puts you in the driver's seat, turning failure from something that happens *to* you into something that happens *for* you.

Take Oprah Winfrey, for example. Before becoming the queen of media, Oprah was fired from her first television job as an evening news anchor. Her producer told her she was "unfit for television." That failure could have crushed her. But instead, Oprah reframed it as a stepping stone. She moved on, found her voice, and built a media empire that transformed the industry.

Failure is only the end if you stop there. If you keep going, it becomes the foundation for your next success. And the more you fail, the better you get at handling it. A 2020 study in *The Journal of Experimental Psychology* found that people who experienced repeated failures developed higher levels of emotional resilience, making them more adaptable and less likely to give up in the face of future challenges.

So here's the bottom line: screw up. Mess up. Take risks that scare you. Fail hard and fail often. Because every failure is an investment in your growth, a step toward something greater.

The next time you fall short, don't see it as a setback. See it as a setup. A setup for learning. A setup for resilience. A setup for success. Because the science of screwing up is clear: failure isn't the opposite of progress—it's the fuel that drives it.

Chapter 8:

Why Perfect Is the Enemy of Progress

Perfectionism sounds noble, doesn't it? The relentless pursuit of excellence, the refusal to settle for less, the drive to create something flawless. It's a trait that's celebrated in job interviews and motivational posters, often mistaken for a key to success. But here's the reality: perfectionism is a prison. It keeps you trapped in an endless loop of procrastination, self-doubt, and, worst of all, inaction.

The irony is that while perfectionism claims to be about getting things right, it usually ends with nothing getting done at all. That's because the pursuit of perfection is inherently unattainable. No matter how much time, energy, or effort you put into something, it can always be better. And so you tweak, revise, and overthink until the deadline passes, the opportunity disappears, or you burn out.

This isn't just anecdotal—it's psychological. A 2018 study published in *Psychological Bulletin* found that rates of perfectionism have significantly increased over the past three decades, fueled in part by societal pressures and the rise of social media. The study also revealed a grim side effect: perfectionism is strongly linked to anxiety, depression, and a crippling fear of failure. The more you chase perfection, the harder it is to move forward.

Take Steve Jobs, for example. When Apple was developing the first Macintosh, Jobs was obsessed with making the computer perfect. He rejected prototypes, demanded impossible design features, and delayed the launch multiple times. While his perfectionism pushed the boundaries of innovation, it also created chaos. Employees burned out, costs skyrocketed, and the project nearly collapsed under its own weight. It wasn't until Jobs learned to balance his pursuit of excellence with practicality that Apple became the powerhouse it is today.

"Chasing perfection is a perfect way to get stuck."

The problem with perfectionism is that it tricks you into believing you need to get everything right before you start. But the truth is, starting is the only way to get things right. Just ask Reid Hoffman, the co-founder of LinkedIn, who famously said, "If you are not embarrassed by the first version of your product, you've launched too late." Hoffman understood that progress is messy, iterative, and far from perfect. The first version of LinkedIn was clunky and basic, but it allowed the team to gather feedback, improve, and grow. If they'd waited for perfection, LinkedIn might never have launched at all.

Here's another example: J.K. Rowling. Before she became one of the best-selling authors in history, Rowling's manuscript for *Harry Potter and the Philosopher's Stone* was rejected by 12 publishers. She could have spent years polishing her book, agonizing over every word, and chasing an unattainable standard of perfection. Instead, she sent it out into the world as it was—imperfect, but good enough. And that "good enough" became a global phenomenon.

The lesson here isn't about settling for mediocrity. It's about understanding that perfection is a myth, and chasing it will only hold you back. Progress, on the other hand, is real. It's tangible. It's achievable. And it only happens when you're willing to take imperfect action.

Think about the Wright brothers. Their first airplane wasn't a sleek, polished machine; it was a shaky, awkward contraption that barely stayed in the air for 12 seconds. But those 12 seconds were enough to change the course of history. They didn't wait for a perfect design. They didn't obsess over every flaw. They built, they tested, they failed, and they tried again. And eventually, they flew.

This concept isn't limited to inventors and entrepreneurs. In 2020, researchers at Stanford University conducted a study on productivity and discovered that people who prioritized action over perfection were 42% more likely to complete their projects. Why? Because they didn't let the fear of imperfection paralyze them. They understood that progress is a process of trial and error, not a quest for flawlessness.

But breaking free from the perfectionist mindset isn't easy. It requires a shift in how you think about failure, success, and your own self-worth. Perfectionism often stems from a fear of being judged, of not measuring up, or of losing control. But the harsh truth is that people are too busy worrying about their own imperfections to notice yours. And even if they do, their judgment says more about them than it does about you.

Consider Thomas Edison, who once said, "I have not failed. I've just found 10,000 ways that won't work." Edison's lightbulb wasn't perfect when he started. It wasn't even functional. But he didn't let that stop him. He kept experimenting, learning, and iterating until he got it right. And the world is brighter—literally—because he was willing to embrace imperfection.

"Done is better than perfect."

— Sheryl Sandberg

In 2015, Sheryl Sandberg, the COO of Facebook, wrote in her book *Lean In* that "done is better than perfect." It's a mantra that challenges the perfectionist mindset, reminding us that completing something imperfectly is infinitely more valuable than never completing it at all. This doesn't mean you should abandon quality or settle for sloppy work. It means you should aim for excellence without letting the impossible standard of perfection hold you back.

So, the next time you find yourself stuck in the endless loop of "not good enough," ask yourself this: What's the worst that could happen if I put this out into the world as it is? Chances are, the answer will be far less catastrophic than you imagine. And even if you stumble, you'll learn, adapt, and grow—because that's what progress looks like.

Perfection might feel safe, but it's a lie. It's the enemy of creativity, productivity, and growth. Progress, on the other hand, is messy, uncertain, and beautifully imperfect. It's the leap before you're ready, the draft before it's polished, the step before the path is clear.

So stop waiting for perfect. Start moving. Start building. Start failing. Because progress is made by those who are brave enough to embrace imperfection—and wise enough to know it's the only way forward.

Chapter 9:

Rejection Is Just Redirection

Rejection has a way of cutting straight to the ego. It doesn't matter if it's a polite no, a ghosted email, or an outright "You're not good enough"—it stings. It feels personal, final, like a verdict on your worth or potential. But here's the truth about rejection: it's not the end. It's a detour, a recalibration, a push toward something better.

To see rejection for what it truly is, you first have to strip it of its emotional baggage. That sting you feel? It's not because rejection is inherently bad; it's because you've attached meaning to it. A 2020 study published in *Nature Communications* found that the human brain processes rejection in the same neural pathways as physical pain. In other words, your brain doesn't distinguish between a bruised ego and a bruised knee—it registers both as "ouch."

But just because rejection feels painful doesn't mean it's harmful. In fact, it can be one of the most constructive experiences in your life, if you let it. The difference lies in how you interpret it.

Take Michael Jordan, often regarded as the greatest basketball player of all time. When he was a sophomore in high school, he didn't make the varsity team. Rejection could have ended his basketball dreams then and there. Instead, he used it as fuel. Jordan later said, "Whenever I was working out and got tired and figured I ought to stop, I'd close my eyes and see that list in the locker room without my name on it." That rejection didn't define him—it redirected him toward greatness.

The same principle applies to countless success stories. Oprah Winfrey was told she wasn't fit for television. Steven Spielberg was rejected by the University of Southern California's film school—twice. J.K. Rowling's manuscript for *Harry Potter* was turned down by 12 publishers. If they had taken rejection as a full stop, their stories would have ended there. Instead, they treated rejection as a comma—a pause, not a period.

"A 'no' doesn't close the door—it points you to the right one."

But rejection doesn't just redirect you toward success; it teaches resilience. In 2014, a team of psychologists at the University of California conducted an experiment on rejection and emotional growth. They found that individuals who experienced repeated rejection were more likely to develop emotional resilience, problem-solving skills, and a greater sense of self-awareness. In other words, rejection toughens you up.

The key to bouncing back from rejection lies in reframing it. Instead of seeing it as evidence of failure, view it as feedback. Ask yourself: What can I learn from this? How can I improve? Sometimes the lesson is about persistence. Other times, it's about pivoting, rethinking your approach, or even pursuing a different path entirely.

Consider Howard Schultz, the man who turned Starbucks into a global coffee empire. Before Starbucks, Schultz pitched his idea for an Italian-style coffeehouse to over 200 investors. He was rejected by nearly every single one of them. But each rejection gave him insight into how to refine his pitch. By the time he found investors willing to take a chance, Schultz had a business plan so solid it couldn't fail.

Rejection also forces you to confront your ego. It's humbling, and that's not a bad thing. Humility opens the door to growth. When you stop seeing rejection as an attack on your worth and start seeing it as an opportunity to learn, you unlock a new level of self-awareness.

Take the music industry. Lady Gaga was dropped by her first record label after only three months. Instead of quitting, she doubled down, honing her style and sound until she became a global icon. Gaga later said, "I had a boyfriend who told me I'd never succeed, never be nominated for a Grammy, never have a hit song, and that he hoped I'd fail. I said to him, 'Someday, when we're not together, you won't be able to order a cup of coffee at the f***ing deli without hearing or seeing me.'" Rejection wasn't her enemy; it was her motivator.

Even in the corporate world, rejection plays a pivotal role. In 2009, Airbnb's founders were rejected by nearly every venture capitalist in Silicon Valley. They were told their idea was too niche, too risky, and too weird. Today, Airbnb is valued at over $100 billion. Every rejection they faced strengthened their resolve and clarified their vision.

But rejection isn't always about proving people wrong. Sometimes, it's about realizing that the path you were on wasn't the right one. Steve Jobs, after being fired from Apple—the company he co-founded—could have wallowed in bitterness. Instead, he used the time away to build NeXT and Pixar, two ventures that eventually led to his triumphant return to Apple. Jobs later said, "Getting fired from Apple was the best thing that could have ever happened to me. The heaviness of being successful was replaced by the lightness of being a beginner again."

"When the door closes, you have two choices: give up, or keep going. And if you're like me, you find a window to climb through."

— Rihanna

Here's the thing about rejection: it forces you to move. Whether that's forward, sideways, or backward, it gets you unstuck. It demands action, reflection, and sometimes reinvention. And in that movement, you find clarity, purpose, and new opportunities you might never have considered otherwise.

So the next time you're faced with rejection—whether it's a missed promotion, a failed pitch, or a breakup—remember this: rejection isn't about you. It's about alignment. It's life's way of saying, "Not here, not now, not this." It's not a door slamming shut; it's a signpost pointing you in a different direction.

The road ahead won't always be smooth, and rejection will never stop stinging entirely. But each no brings you closer to the yes that matters. Rejection isn't the enemy. It's just redirection. And it's up to you to decide where it takes you.

Chapter 10:

How to Turn a Faceplant Into a Launchpad

Failure often feels like hitting a brick wall. The plans you meticulously crafted have crumbled, your confidence is in shambles, and all that's left is the sinking realization that you've failed. But what if that crash wasn't the end of the road? What if it was the beginning of something bigger, something better? The truth is, the greatest successes often emerge from the ashes of failure. But to rise, you have to stop seeing failure as a fall and start treating it as a launchpad.

It's easy to dwell on the fall. After all, it's what we're conditioned to do. Society rewards success and punishes failure, framing it as an outcome to avoid at all costs. But the stories we celebrate—the billion-dollar startups, the legendary artists, the game-changing leaders—are often born from spectacular failures. The key isn't avoiding failure; it's learning how to leverage it.

Take the story of Walt Disney. Before becoming synonymous with creativity and imagination, Disney faced a series of crushing failures. His first animation company went bankrupt. He was fired from a newspaper job because his editor claimed he "lacked imagination." Even after creating Mickey Mouse, Disney struggled to secure funding for his projects, including *Snow White and the Seven Dwarfs*, which many predicted would ruin him. But Disney didn't let his failures define him. Instead, he used them to refine his vision, build resilience, and take risks that ultimately changed entertainment forever.

Science backs up the idea that failure can be transformative. A 2019 study published in *Nature Communications* examined the trajectories of over 700,000 scientists. Researchers found that those who experienced early career failures were more likely to achieve major breakthroughs later on than those who had early successes. The reason? Failure forces you to adapt. It sharpens your problem-solving skills, boosts creativity, and strengthens your resilience. Success, on the other hand, often breeds complacency.

"Faceplants aren't failures; they're floor-level opportunities to rise."

Consider the tech industry, where failure is practically a rite of passage. In 2001, Apple released the Power Mac G4 Cube, a sleek and innovative computer that flopped miserably. Consumers found it too expensive and impractical, and it was discontinued within a year. For most companies, a failure like that could have been devastating. But Apple didn't retreat; they learned. The Cube's design principles laid the groundwork for future successes, including the Mac Mini and the iPod. What looked like a faceplant at the time became a stepping stone to innovation.

The same principle applies on a personal level. Think about the times in your life when you've failed. Maybe it was a relationship that ended badly, a job you didn't get, or a goal you didn't achieve. Now think about what happened next. Did you learn something about yourself? Did you change your approach? Did that failure redirect you toward something better? If you're honest, the answer is probably yes.

Failure has a way of clarifying what matters. It strips away the noise and forces you to focus on the essentials. When things go wrong, you're left with a choice: give up or start again. The process isn't easy—it's messy, uncomfortable, and often painful. But it's also where growth happens.

Look at Oprah Winfrey, who was fired from her first television job and told she was "unfit for TV." That rejection could have ended her career before it began. Instead, it pushed her to find her voice and redefine her path. Today, Oprah isn't just a media mogul; she's a cultural icon. Her failures didn't hold her back—they propelled her forward.

So how do you turn your own faceplants into launchpads? Start by reframing failure. Instead of seeing it as a verdict on your abilities, see it as feedback. Ask yourself: What went wrong? What can I do differently next time? Be brutally honest but also compassionate. Failure isn't an indictment of your worth; it's a sign that you tried, that you put yourself out there.

Next, take action. Reflection is important, but it's only the first step. The real magic happens when you use what you've learned to move forward. Think about Sarah Blakely, the founder of Spanx. Before becoming a billionaire, Blakely failed the LSAT twice and worked as a fax machine salesperson. But those experiences taught her resilience, creativity, and the value of persistence—lessons that helped her revolutionize the shapewear industry. Blakely often credits her failures as the foundation of her success.

"Rock bottom became the solid foundation on which I rebuilt my life."

— J.K. Rowling

Failure also demands adaptability. Sometimes, the path you're on isn't the right one. Failure forces you to pivot, to explore alternatives you might not have considered otherwise. In 2008, Airbnb's founders were on the verge of giving up. Their idea—a platform for renting air mattresses—wasn't gaining traction. Desperate, they pivoted, focusing on creating a seamless booking experience for all kinds of accommodations. That shift turned Airbnb into a multi-billion-dollar company.

And then there's the power of persistence. Failure isn't a one-and-done deal. You'll fall again, and again, and again. The difference between those who succeed and those who don't isn't the absence of failure—it's the refusal to give up. Take Colonel Harland Sanders, who founded KFC at the age of 65 after being rejected over 1,000 times when pitching his fried chicken recipe. His story is a testament to the power of perseverance.

Of course, not every failure leads to immediate success. Sometimes, the lessons aren't clear right away. Sometimes, it feels like you're stuck in a cycle of setbacks. But even then, failure is working for you. It's building your resilience, sharpening your skills, and preparing you for the opportunities ahead.

The next time you faceplant, resist the urge to retreat. Instead, lean in. Reflect, adapt, and keep moving. Remember that failure isn't a dead end—it's a launchpad. It's the starting point for something bigger, something better. And while the fall might hurt, the rise will always be worth it.

The Emotional Cycle of Failure

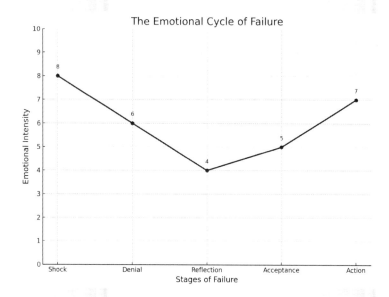

This chart maps the emotional journey through failure, from the initial shock to eventual action. While emotions peak early with shock and denial, they gradually stabilize during reflection and acceptance, culminating in a renewed sense of purpose through action.

Chapter 11:

Laughing at Your Ls (And Why You Shouldn't Take Yourself Too Seriously)

Failure has a way of feeling larger than life. When things go wrong, it's easy to fall into a spiral of self-pity and despair, as if the universe conspired to humiliate you personally. But what if, instead of treating your failures like tragedies, you treated them like punchlines? What if, instead of running from your mistakes, you laughed at them?

This isn't about minimizing the importance of failure or ignoring its lessons. It's about reclaiming the power it often takes from you. Humor has a unique ability to take the sting out of failure, to put things into perspective, and to remind you that life isn't as serious as it seems.

The science backs this up. A 2020 study published in the *Journal of Experimental Psychology* found that individuals who used humor to cope with failure experienced lower levels of stress and higher levels of resilience. The act of laughing—even at your own expense—reduces cortisol (the stress hormone) and triggers the release of endorphins, creating a sense of relief and optimism. In short, laughing at your Ls doesn't just feel good; it's scientifically proven to help you bounce back faster.

Take Jennifer Lawrence, for example. During the 2013 Oscars, Lawrence tripped on her way to accept her Best Actress award. The moment could have been mortifying, but instead of letting it define her night, she laughed it off. When a reporter later asked her about the fall, she quipped, "You guys are just standing up because you feel bad that I fell—and that's really embarrassing." That moment of self-deprecating humor endeared her to millions and proved that even under the brightest spotlight, it's possible to own your mistakes with grace and laughter.

Self-deprecation isn't just about deflecting embarrassment; it's a tool for resilience. By acknowledging your failures with humor, you strip them of their power to intimidate or define you. You remind yourself—and everyone else—that you're human, fallible, and capable of finding the funny side of even the worst situations.

"If you can laugh at your failures, you've already won half the battle."

Consider the story of Thomas Edison, who famously said, "I have not failed. I've just found 10,000 ways that won't work." Edison's humor wasn't just a way of brushing off his failures; it was a mindset that allowed him to keep going. Each misstep became part of the process, not an indictment of his abilities. By reframing failure as something almost comically inevitable, Edison freed himself from the fear of it.

Humor also has a way of bringing people together. When you're honest and lighthearted about your mistakes, you create space for others to do the same. Think about the workplace. A boss who admits their own missteps and laughs at themselves fosters a culture of openness and collaboration. In contrast, a leader who pretends to be infallible creates an environment of fear, where employees are afraid to take risks or own up to their mistakes.

Take Elon Musk, a figure often associated with audacious risk-taking and larger-than-life ideas. When Tesla faced criticism over production delays and quality issues, Musk didn't shy away from the jokes. Instead, he joined in, tweeting memes and acknowledging the company's growing pains with humor. This transparency and willingness to laugh at his own challenges strengthened his connection with supporters and humanized his brand.

The ability to laugh at failure isn't just for celebrities and CEOs; it's a skill anyone can cultivate. It starts with perspective. Ask yourself: Will this matter in five years? Five months? Five minutes? More often than not, the answer is no. What feels catastrophic in the moment usually fades into the background with time—and, if you let it, becomes a funny story to tell later.

Think about your own life. How many of your most embarrassing moments are now the ones you laugh about with friends? The disastrous date, the awkward presentation, the time you accidentally hit "Reply All" on an email—these moments felt unbearable at the time, but now they're stories that bring people together.

Take failure as a chance to create those stories. Consider Sara Blakely, the billionaire founder of Spanx. Early in her career, she sold fax machines door-to-door—a job she was terrible at. Blakely often tells stories about her hilarious missteps, from awkward sales pitches to being chased off porches by angry homeowners. Instead of hiding her failures, she embraces them, using humor to connect with her audience and illustrate the value of persistence.

"Success is stumbling from failure to failure with no loss of enthusiasm"

— Winston Churchill

There's also a deeper power in humor: it forces you to let go of perfectionism. When you laugh at your mistakes, you acknowledge that you don't have it all figured out—and that's okay. Perfection is an illusion, and clinging to it only makes failure feel heavier.

Take a cue from Winston Churchill, who once said, "Success is going from failure to failure without loss of enthusiasm." Churchill wasn't advocating for blind optimism; he was reminding us that failure is a natural part of the process—and that keeping a sense of humor can make the journey bearable.

But what about those failures that don't feel funny? The ones that hit hard and leave you questioning everything? Even then, humor can be a lifeline. It might not come immediately, but over time, finding the absurdity in a tough situation can help you move forward. Laughter doesn't erase the pain, but it lightens the load, making it easier to carry.

Think about the 2008 financial crisis, which left countless entrepreneurs struggling to stay afloat. One such entrepreneur was Ben Huh, founder of the popular humor site I Can Has Cheezburger. Huh was nearly bankrupt when he decided to lean into humor, doubling down on the idea that people needed laughter more than ever. His decision not only saved his business but also proved that even in the darkest times, humor has a role to play.

So, the next time you stumble, fall, or outright fail, resist the urge to take it too seriously. Find the humor in the situation, even if it's just a small, absurd detail. Share your story with someone who'll laugh with you. Remind yourself that this moment, no matter how painful, is temporary—and that someday, it might even make a great punchline.

Because here's the truth: life is messy, unpredictable, and often ridiculous. Failure is inevitable, but it doesn't have to define you. Laughing at your Ls doesn't mean you're dismissing their significance; it means you're refusing to let them own you. And in that laughter, you'll find the strength to pick yourself up, dust yourself off, and keep going. After all, every great story needs a little comic relief.

Chapter 12:

The "What If" Trap: Escaping Paralysis by Analysis

"What if I fail?" "What if I'm not good enough?" "What if this ruins everything?"

If these questions sound familiar, you're not alone. The "what if" trap is a universal mental game—a vicious loop of hypothetical fears and worst-case scenarios that paralyze action and feed indecision. It's the quiet voice that whispers doubt when you're standing on the edge of a leap. And while it might feel like you're being cautious, this overthinking is often the very thing holding you back.

The truth is, the "what if" trap isn't about solving problems; it's about avoiding them. It's a defense mechanism, a way for your brain to keep you safe by creating imaginary hurdles so you never leave your comfort zone. But safety is a double-edged sword. What keeps you protected also keeps you stagnant.

Psychologists have a term for this: *paralysis by analysis.* It happens when the act of overthinking becomes so overwhelming that it prevents you from making decisions or taking action. A 2020 study published in *Personality and Social Psychology Review* found that people who ruminate excessively are significantly less likely to follow through on their goals, regardless of their intentions or capabilities. In essence, the more you think about "what if," the less likely you are to find out "what is."

Take Jeff Bezos, founder of Amazon. In the early 1990s, Bezos was a high-ranking executive at a hedge fund, earning a stable and lucrative salary. When he came up with the idea for an online bookstore, he faced a cascade of "what if" questions: What if it fails? What if he loses his savings? What if he ruins his career? Instead of letting those questions paralyze him, Bezos developed a concept he called the "regret minimization framework." He asked himself, "When I'm 80 years old, will I regret not trying?" The answer was clear. He left his job, started Amazon in his garage, and built one of the most successful companies in history.

Bezos didn't ignore the "what ifs"; he reframed them. He focused not on the fear of failure, but on the fear of regret. This shift in perspective is crucial. Fear of failure might keep you from trying, but regret for not trying is far more permanent.

"Most of the things you're afraid of will never happen—so stop waiting and start trying."

This same principle applies across industries and disciplines. Consider Vera Wang, now one of the world's most renowned fashion designers. Wang started her career as a figure skater, then transitioned to journalism, working as an editor at *Vogue*. At age 40, she faced a life-defining decision: stay in her stable career or take a risk and enter the competitive world of fashion design. The "what ifs" were endless, but Wang chose to move forward. Today, she's a global icon, proving that sometimes the scariest decisions lead to the most rewarding outcomes.

But how do you escape the "what if" trap when it feels all-consuming? The first step is recognizing that most of the fears it presents are baseless. A study from Cornell University found that 85% of what people worry about never actually happens. Of the remaining 15%, the majority of outcomes are either manageable or less catastrophic than imagined. In short, your brain is an expert at creating problems that don't exist.

The second step is embracing imperfection. Perfectionism and the "what if" trap often go hand in hand. The fear of not doing something perfectly can stop you from doing it at all. But progress isn't about perfection—it's about momentum. Consider Howard Schultz, the former CEO of Starbucks. When Schultz first pitched his vision for transforming Starbucks from a coffee bean supplier into a café chain, he faced relentless criticism. Investors questioned the scalability of his idea and the public's willingness to pay premium prices for coffee. Schultz didn't have all the answers, and his execution wasn't flawless, but he moved forward anyway. Today, Starbucks has over 35,000 locations worldwide.

Another powerful antidote to the "what if" trap is action. Even small steps can break the cycle of overthinking. In 2015, Shonda Rhimes, the powerhouse producer behind hits like *Grey's Anatomy* and *Scandal*, wrote *Year of Yes*, a memoir detailing her decision to say "yes" to opportunities that scared her. Rhimes had spent years letting "what if" fears hold her back—what if she embarrassed herself? What if she failed in public? By committing to action, she shattered the mental barriers that had confined her. The result wasn't just professional growth but personal transformation.

Action doesn't have to be bold or dramatic; it just has to be deliberate. If you're considering starting a business, your first step isn't launching a full-blown company—it's researching the market. If you want to switch careers, your first step isn't quitting your job—it's updating your résumé. The simple act of doing something, anything, breaks the inertia of indecision and sets you on a path forward.

"Worrying is like a rocking chair. It gives you something to do but gets you nowhere."

— Glenn Turner

Perspective also matters. Olympic champion Michael Phelps has often spoken about the power of visualization in his training. Before each race, Phelps mentally rehearses every possible scenario, including things going wrong: a bad start, water in his goggles, or an unexpected surge from a competitor. By confronting these "what if" scenarios head-on, Phelps prepares himself not to avoid failure, but to navigate it. This mindset has helped him win 23 gold medals, even when things didn't go perfectly.

The final piece of escaping the "what if" trap is accepting uncertainty. Life is unpredictable. No amount of planning, analysis, or overthinking can eliminate risk. But that's not a reason to stand still; it's a reason to move. Uncertainty isn't the enemy—it's the backdrop against which every meaningful achievement unfolds.

Take Jamie Kern Lima, the founder of IT Cosmetics. Lima spent years pitching her product to investors, only to face rejection after rejection. Industry experts told her that her vision didn't align with consumer trends and that her brand was doomed to fail. But Lima refused to let the "what ifs" win. She persevered, eventually selling IT Cosmetics to L'Oréal for $1.2 billion and becoming the company's first female CEO.

The "what if" trap is insidious, but it's not unbeatable. Every time you find yourself spiraling into hypothetical fears, pause and ask yourself: What's the worst that could happen? More often than not, the answer will be far less catastrophic than you think. And even if the worst does happen, you'll survive. You'll adapt. You'll grow.

So take the leap. Make the call. Write the first chapter. Whatever it is you're holding back on, stop letting "what if" run the show. Because the real question isn't "What if I fail?" It's "What if I succeed?" And the only way to find out is to try.

Chapter 13:

Bounce Back Like a Boss: Resilience 101

Resilience. It's one of those words that sounds good in theory but feels impossible to embody when life knocks you flat. When the job doesn't come through, the relationship falls apart, or the big idea crashes and burns, resilience feels like something reserved for other people—the ones who seem to have it all figured out. But here's the truth: resilience isn't a gift. It's a skill. And like any skill, it can be learned, practiced, and strengthened.

The ability to bounce back isn't about being unbreakable; it's about being adaptable. Resilience doesn't mean you don't feel pain, frustration, or disappointment. It means you don't let those feelings define you. You feel them, process them, and move forward anyway.

Consider the story of Nelson Mandela. After spending 27 years in prison for fighting apartheid, Mandela could have emerged bitter, broken, and defeated. Instead, he chose reconciliation over revenge, leading South Africa into a new era of democracy and becoming a global symbol of resilience. Mandela's strength didn't come from ignoring his suffering; it came from using it as a foundation for growth.

Psychologists often describe resilience as a combination of two factors: adaptability and grit. Adaptability is your ability to adjust to new circumstances, while grit is your ability to keep going in the face of challenges. Together, these traits create a mindset that thrives on perseverance and problem-solving. A 2017 study published in *Psychological Science* found that individuals who scored high in both adaptability and grit were 45% more likely to achieve long-term success, even after experiencing significant setbacks.

But how do you cultivate resilience in your own life? It starts with perspective. When things go wrong, it's easy to spiral into self-pity and despair. "Why me?" becomes the dominant question, and the world starts to feel like a hostile, unfair place. The first step to resilience is flipping that script. Instead of asking, "Why me?" ask, "What now?" Shifting your focus from blame to action helps you regain a sense of control.

"Resilience isn't about never falling; it's about always getting back up."

Take Serena Williams, one of the greatest athletes of all time. In 2017, Williams experienced a life-threatening pulmonary embolism after giving birth to her daughter. The recovery process was grueling, both physically and emotionally. But instead of giving up, Williams used her experience to fuel her comeback. She returned to professional tennis and reached multiple Grand Slam finals, proving that resilience is as much about determination as it is about recovery.

Resilience also requires community. No one bounces back alone. A strong support network—whether it's friends, family, or mentors—provides the encouragement and perspective needed to move forward. In 2010, after a devastating earthquake struck Haiti, the country's resilience was tested on an unimaginable scale. Communities came together, supporting one another through the aftermath and rebuilding process. That collective strength showed the power of connection in overcoming adversity.

Another critical aspect of resilience is learning to embrace failure. It sounds counterintuitive, but failure is often the best teacher. In 1975, Bill Gates co-founded a company called Traf-O-Data, which aimed to process traffic data for local governments. The business failed miserably. But Gates took the lessons he learned from that failure and applied them to his next venture—Microsoft. Today, he's one of the wealthiest and most successful entrepreneurs in history. Gates didn't let failure define him; he let it refine him.

Building resilience also means taking care of yourself. Physical health and mental health are deeply interconnected, and neglecting one often harms the other. A 2018 study from the *Journal of Health Psychology* found that regular exercise and mindfulness practices significantly improve resilience by reducing stress and increasing emotional regulation. It's not about running marathons or meditating for hours; even small, consistent habits—like a daily walk or a five-minute breathing exercise—can make a difference.

But resilience isn't just about surviving challenges; it's about thriving in their aftermath. That means finding meaning in your struggles and using them as a catalyst for growth. Viktor Frankl, a Holocaust survivor and author of *Man's Search for Meaning*, argued that our ability to endure hardship depends on our ability to find purpose in it. Frankl wrote, "When we are no longer able to change a situation, we are challenged to change ourselves."

"Do not judge me by my success, judge me by how many times I fell down and got back up again."

— Nelson Mandela

This idea of finding purpose in pain is echoed in the story of Malala Yousafzai. After being shot by the Taliban for advocating girls' education, Malala could have retreated into fear and silence. Instead, she became a global activist, winning the Nobel Peace Prize at age 17 and continuing to fight for education equality.

Her resilience transformed personal tragedy into global impact.

So how can you apply these lessons to your own life? Start by recognizing that resilience isn't about avoiding hardship; it's about responding to it. When setbacks happen—and they will—give yourself permission to feel the disappointment. But don't stay there. Reflect on what went wrong, what you can learn, and what steps you can take to move forward.

Surround yourself with people who lift you up, not drag you down. Seek out mentors who've faced similar challenges and come out stronger. Remember that asking for help isn't a sign of weakness; it's a sign of strength.

And finally, remind yourself that resilience is a journey, not a destination. It's a skill you'll use again and again, refining it with each new challenge. Every setback is an opportunity to practice bouncing back, to prove to yourself that you're stronger, braver, and more capable than you think.

Resilience doesn't mean you won't fall—it means you'll always get back up. And with each bounce, you'll climb higher, turning every stumble into a stepping stone for success.

Chapter 14: The Social Media Myth: Success Isn't Always Sexy

In a world where a single Instagram post can launch a career or a viral TikTok can make someone famous overnight, it's easy to believe that success should be instant, effortless, and picture-perfect. Scroll through your feed, and you'll see influencers flaunting luxurious lifestyles, entrepreneurs announcing record-breaking sales, and artists unveiling their latest masterpieces. It's intoxicating—and completely misleading.

Social media has created a myth of success: that it's linear, glamorous, and free from struggle. But here's the truth: behind every highlight reel is a story of late nights, self-doubt, and countless failures that never make it to the screen. The problem isn't just that these stories are invisible; it's that their absence creates unrealistic expectations for everyone else.

Take Ed Sheeran, now one of the most famous musicians in the world. Before his rise to fame, Sheeran spent years playing tiny venues and sleeping on friends' couches. He performed at open mic nights where no one listened and handed out CDs on the streets. None of this was glamorous, and none of it made it to social media. But those unsexy, grinding years were the foundation for his success. Without them, the polished performances you see today wouldn't exist.

The myth of effortless success isn't just misleading—it's harmful. A 2019 study published in the

Journal of Social and Clinical Psychology found that heavy social media use is strongly linked to feelings of inadequacy and depression, particularly when users compare their lives to the curated content they see online. The constant exposure to other people's "perfect" moments creates a distorted sense of reality, making your own struggles feel like failures.

But the truth is, struggle is not the exception; it's the rule. Success isn't sexy. It's messy, complicated, and often boring. It's the countless hours of hard work that no one sees, the setbacks that feel insurmountable, and the decisions that make you question everything. Social media doesn't show the writer staring at a blank page for hours, the entrepreneur hustling to make rent, or the athlete pushing through injury and exhaustion. But those moments are where success is built.

"Behind every 'overnight success' is a decade of unseen grind."

Consider Sara Blakely, the founder of Spanx. Blakely started her company with $5,000 in savings, selling shapewear out of her apartment. She faced rejection after rejection from manufacturers who didn't believe in her product. For two years, she worked her day job selling fax machines while building Spanx at night.

There were no viral moments, no overnight wins—just persistence, resilience, and a willingness to endure the grind. Today, Spanx is a billion-dollar brand, but the path to get there was anything but glamorous.

The tech industry tells a similar story. Elon Musk, now synonymous with innovation, spent years in relative obscurity working on startups like Zip2 and X.com (which eventually became PayPal). His early ventures were riddled with challenges, including near bankruptcy and public skepticism. The viral images of Musk unveiling Tesla's Cybertruck or SpaceX's Falcon Heavy launch are the results of decades of struggle, not spontaneous genius.

The myth of social media success also ignores one critical truth: not everything that glitters is gold. Many of the successes you see online are exaggerated, curated, or outright fake. A 2020 investigation by *The New York Times* revealed that some influencers rent private jets for staged photos, pretending to lead luxurious lifestyles they can't afford. Others buy followers, likes, and comments to create the illusion of popularity. This facade perpetuates the idea that success should be effortless, leaving the rest of us wondering what we're doing wrong.

But the reality is, success takes time. A 2014 study by the National Bureau of Economic Research analyzed 11,000 entrepreneurs and found that the average age of a successful startup founder was 45—not 25, as the tech world often suggests. Success is rarely a sprint; it's a marathon. It requires patience, perseverance, and a willingness to endure the mundane, unglamorous work that no one sees.

The entertainment industry offers another lens on this reality. Viola Davis, one of the most acclaimed actresses of her generation, didn't achieve mainstream success until her 40s. Before that, she spent decades honing her craft in theater, taking small roles in film and television, and facing the harsh realities of an industry that often overlooks Black actresses. Davis has spoken openly about the struggles she endured and the persistence it took to get where she is today. Her story is a powerful reminder that success isn't about instant gratification—it's about staying the course.

"Don't compare your Chapter 1 to someone else's Chapter 20."

— Jon Acuff

So why do we buy into the myth? Part of the answer lies in our biology. Humans are wired to seek shortcuts. We love the idea of overnight success because it appeals to our desire for efficiency and reward. Social media feeds into this by presenting only the highlights, creating a distorted view of what success actually looks like.

But if you dig deeper, you'll find that every "overnight success" was years in the making. Beyoncé, often seen as a pinnacle of talent and achievement, spent her childhood rehearsing for hours every day. She performed at local talent shows, suffered losses, and faced rejection long before becoming a global icon. Her success wasn't handed to her; it was earned through relentless hard work.

The next time you find yourself scrolling through social media, feeling like everyone else has it figured out, pause. Remind yourself that what you're seeing is a highlight reel, not the full story. Behind every glossy post is a reality far messier—and far more relatable—than you realize.

Success isn't always sexy, and that's okay. The unfiltered version of success—the late nights, the sacrifices, the failures—is what makes it real. It's what makes it meaningful. And it's what makes it yours. So stop comparing your behind-the-scenes to someone else's highlight reel. Embrace the grind, the struggle, and the imperfections. Because that's where the real story begins.

Risk Tolerance by Age Group

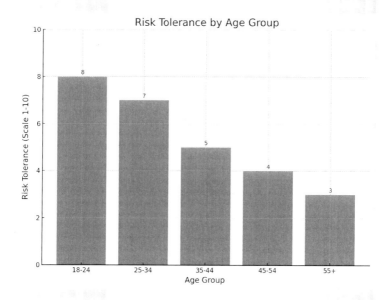

This chart shows how risk tolerance typically declines with age. Younger groups are more willing to take risks, driven by fewer responsibilities and a longer time horizon, while older groups prioritize stability and calculated decisions.

Chapter 15:

Fail Harder, Love Smarter: Risks in Relationships

When people talk about risk, they're usually thinking about business ventures, career moves, or creative projects. Rarely do they consider the biggest risk of all: love. Relationships—whether romantic, platonic, or familial—are a gamble every time. You're putting your heart, your time, and your trust on the line with no guarantee that it will work out. And yet, we take the risk because the alternative—living without connection—is far more dangerous.

Love is messy. It doesn't follow a five-year plan or a predictable trajectory. There are no metrics for success, no quarterly reviews to tell you if you're doing it right. That's what makes it so terrifying—and so rewarding. A 2017 study published in the *Journal of Positive Psychology* found that strong relationships are one of the most significant predictors of happiness and life satisfaction. But those relationships don't come without effort, and they certainly don't come without failure.

"Love is the ultimate risk—and the ultimate reward."

Take Ruth Bader Ginsburg, the late Supreme Court Justice, as an example. Ginsburg often spoke about the role her husband, Marty, played in her life. Their relationship wasn't perfect—no relationship is—but it was a partnership rooted in mutual respect and support. When Ruth's career took off, Marty stepped back from his own ambitions to ensure she could thrive. Their marriage was a testament to the risks and rewards of love: the willingness to adapt, to sacrifice, and to fail together.

Failure in relationships is inevitable. People fight, drift apart, and make mistakes. The key isn't avoiding these moments but learning from them. Consider Michelle and Barack Obama, who have spoken candidly about the challenges in their marriage. In their book and interviews, they've acknowledged periods of tension and misalignment, particularly during Barack's early political career. Instead of letting those challenges define their relationship, they used them as opportunities to grow individually and as a couple.

Resilience in relationships mirrors resilience in other areas of life. It's about showing up, even when things are hard. It's about listening, even when you're hurt. And it's about forgiving, even when it feels easier to hold a grudge. A 2018 study from the *Journal of Family Psychology* found that couples who viewed conflict as an opportunity for growth were significantly more likely to stay together and report higher relationship satisfaction than those who avoided addressing their issues.

But not every relationship is meant to last, and that's okay. Sometimes, failure in love isn't about working harder—it's about knowing when to walk away. Take the story of Maya Angelou, who divorced three times before finding her stride as a single, independent woman. Angelou didn't view her divorces as failures but as necessary steps in her journey to self-discovery. She once said, "Have enough courage to trust love one more time and always one more time."

Walking away from a relationship can feel like the ultimate failure, but it's often a necessary act of self-respect. In 2021, a *Harvard Business Review* article explored the concept of "relationship ROI," suggesting that not all relationships provide a return on the emotional investment required to sustain them. Letting go isn't a sign of weakness; it's a recognition of what you need to thrive.

"Love is a risk. It's one that always yields either the greatest reward or the greatest lesson."

— Demi Lovato

Friendships carry their own set of risks and rewards. Think about Oprah Winfrey and Gayle King, whose decades-long friendship has been a cornerstone of both their lives. They've openly discussed moments of conflict, including times when jealousy and miscommunication tested their bond. Instead of letting those moments drive them apart, they doubled down on honesty and vulnerability, proving that even the strongest friendships require work—and sometimes failure—to survive.

But what about familial relationships? These are often the hardest to navigate because they're rooted in expectations and traditions that can feel impossible to change. Take the story of Warren Buffett, who has been open about his complicated relationship with his late father. Despite their differences, Buffett found ways to honor their connection while forging his own path. His story highlights the importance of setting boundaries and accepting that not every relationship will look the way you hoped.

One of the biggest risks in relationships is vulnerability. Brene Brown, a researcher and author known for her work on vulnerability and shame, describes vulnerability as "uncertainty, risk, and emotional exposure." It's telling someone how you really feel, even when you're scared of rejection. It's admitting you're wrong, even when your ego is screaming at you to hold your ground. And it's loving someone fully, knowing they might not love you back in the same way.

But here's the paradox: vulnerability, the very thing we fear will lead to failure, is what makes relationships thrive. A 2013 study published in *Emotion* found that people who practiced vulnerability in their relationships reported greater intimacy, trust, and overall satisfaction. Vulnerability isn't a weakness; it's a superpower.

And yet, love doesn't always feel like a superpower. It feels like late-night arguments, unanswered texts, and moments of unbearable doubt. It feels like giving your all to someone who might not appreciate it and risking your heart knowing it could be broken. But those moments of failure aren't the end—they're the foundation for growth.

Think about the story of Nelson Mandela and Winnie Mandela. Their marriage endured the strain of apartheid, Mandela's 27 years in prison, and political turmoil. Ultimately, they divorced, but their relationship—flawed and complicated—was a testament to the risks and resilience of love. It wasn't perfect, but it was real, and it shaped both their lives in profound ways.

The truth is, love isn't about avoiding failure; it's about embracing it. It's about showing up, even when you're scared. It's about trying, even when you've been hurt before. And it's about knowing that every failed relationship, every argument, and every heartbreak teaches you something valuable—about yourself, about others, and about what it means to truly connect.

So take the risk. Say the thing you've been afraid to say. Apologize when you're wrong. Let someone in, even if it terrifies you. Love is messy, unpredictable, and guaranteed to include failure. But it's also the most meaningful risk you'll ever take. And if you're willing to fail harder, you just might love smarter.

Chapter 16:

Burnout and Blowups: Learning to Start Again

Burnout isn't just being tired. It's not something you can fix with a weekend off or a good night's sleep. Burnout is waking up one day and realizing that something inside you has run dry, that the spark you once had for your work, your goals, or even your life has been smothered. It's feeling trapped in a cycle of doing and doing, yet somehow feeling like you're going nowhere. And for all the motivational speeches about grit and persistence, burnout is often the result of pushing too hard for too long without ever stopping to ask, "Is this sustainable?"

In 2019, the World Health Organization officially classified burnout as an occupational phenomenon, defining it as a syndrome resulting from chronic workplace stress that hasn't been successfully managed. It's characterized by exhaustion, cynicism, and a sense of reduced accomplishment. A 2021 study by Gallup found that 76% of employees experience burnout at least sometimes, and nearly 28% experience it "very often" or "always." And yet, in a culture that glorifies hustle and endless productivity, burnout is often seen as a personal failing rather than a systemic problem.

But burnout doesn't mean you're weak. It means you've been human in a world that often demands more than humans can give. It's not about laziness or a lack of ambition—it's about the unsustainable pace at which you've been running. And the first step to starting again is admitting that burnout isn't something to be powered through; it's something to be recovered from.

Take the story of Arianna Huffington, founder of *The Huffington Post*. In 2007, Huffington collapsed from exhaustion, hitting her head on her desk and breaking her cheekbone. At the time, she was running one of the most influential media companies in the world, but her relentless schedule had pushed her past her limits. That incident forced Huffington to reevaluate her priorities and approach to work. She became an advocate for well-being, writing books on the importance of sleep and mindfulness. Her burnout wasn't the end—it was the wake-up call she needed to start again with a healthier perspective.

"Burnout isn't a failure; it's your body and mind demanding a reset."

Starting again often requires blowing things up—not literally, but metaphorically. It means dismantling the habits, routines, and expectations that led to burnout in the first place. It's scary to step back, to admit that the path you've been on isn't working, and to choose something different. But sometimes, that's the only way forward.

Consider the story of Howard Schultz, who returned as CEO of Starbucks in 2008 after stepping down years earlier. The company was struggling, having lost sight of its core values in the pursuit of rapid expansion. Schultz made the controversial decision to close all 7,100 U.S. Starbucks locations for one day to retrain baristas on the art of making espresso. Critics called it a PR stunt, but Schultz knew the company needed to hit pause and start again. The move paid off, reigniting Starbucks' brand and profitability. Schultz's willingness to blow up the status quo and refocus on what mattered most saved the company.

Burnout isn't limited to corporate executives and high-profile entrepreneurs. It happens to teachers, nurses, artists, and parents. It happens to anyone who cares deeply about what they do and feels the weight of unrelenting pressure. And while burnout can feel like a failure, it's often a sign that you've been trying too hard to meet expectations that aren't sustainable—or even realistic.

In 2017, Simone Biles, the most decorated gymnast in history, made headlines when she chose to prioritize her mental health over competing in the Tokyo Olympics. Biles faced intense criticism, but her decision sparked a global conversation about the importance of stepping back before burnout leads to permanent damage. Biles later said, "I have to focus on my mental health and not jeopardize my health and well-being." Her choice to step away wasn't weakness; it was courage. And it showed the world that starting again sometimes means pressing pause.

But what does starting again look like for the rest of us? For many, it begins with redefining success. A 2018 study by the *American Psychological Association* found that people who based their self-worth solely on their achievements were more likely to experience burnout and depression than those who valued relationships, personal growth, or leisure activities. Success doesn't have to mean climbing higher and faster—it can mean finding balance, setting boundaries, and creating a life that feels meaningful.

"Almost everything will work again if you unplug it for a few minutes, including you."

— Anne Lamott

Burnout also forces you to confront the question: What do I actually want? It's easy to get caught up in chasing goals that don't align with your values because they look good on paper or fit someone else's definition of success. Starting again means reevaluating those goals and giving yourself permission to change course.

Take the story of Elizabeth Gilbert, author of *Eat, Pray, Love*. After the massive success of her book, Gilbert felt enormous pressure to replicate that achievement. The weight of expectation led her to step away from traditional publishing for a time, focusing instead on smaller, more personal projects. Gilbert has spoken openly about how redefining her relationship with success allowed her to rediscover her love for writing.

Recovery from burnout isn't linear. It's messy, frustrating, and often slow. But it's also transformative. It teaches you to listen to your body and mind, to recognize when you're approaching your limits, and to prioritize rest and renewal. It's about learning to say no, even when it feels uncomfortable, and to let go of the guilt that comes with stepping back.

Ultimately, burnout isn't just about work—it's about how we live. It's about the stories we tell ourselves about worth, productivity, and success. It's about the pressure to always be "on," always be achieving, and never admit that we're struggling. But starting again means rewriting those stories. It means choosing a life that's not just about doing, but about being.

Burnout and blowups aren't the end of the line—they're the turning points that force us to reevaluate, recalibrate, and begin anew. Starting again is never easy, but it's always worth it. Because sometimes, the best way forward is to stop, reflect, and choose a different path.

Chapter 17:

Imposter Syndrome: Why Everyone's Wingin' It

You've probably felt it before. That gnawing sense that you don't belong. That someone, somewhere, is going to figure out you're not as smart, talented, or capable as they think you are. Maybe it crept in during a job interview, while leading a team, or even during a conversation where everyone else seemed more confident, more knowledgeable, more "together." That feeling has a name: imposter syndrome.

Imposter syndrome is the psychological phenomenon where people doubt their abilities and feel like frauds, despite evidence to the contrary. It's a voice in your head that says, *You don't deserve to be here.* And here's the kicker: it's a liar.

The first thing you need to know about imposter syndrome is that it's universal. A 2020 study by the International Journal of Behavioral Science found that 70% of people experience imposter syndrome at some point in their lives. It doesn't matter if you're a student, a CEO, or a Nobel Prize winner—no one is immune. Even people at the top of their game, the ones who seem untouchable, wrestle with self-doubt.

Take Maya Angelou. Despite her towering achievements as a writer, poet, and civil rights activist, Angelou often felt like a fraud. She once admitted, "I have written eleven books, but each time I think, 'Uh oh, they're going to find out now. I've run a game on everybody, and they're going to find me out.'" If Maya Angelou felt like an imposter, what does that say about the rest of us?

Even Albert Einstein wasn't exempt. Near the end of his life, Einstein described himself as "an involuntary swindler," believing his fame and accolades were out of proportion to his actual achievements. Imagine that: the man whose name is synonymous with genius doubted himself. If that doesn't tell you how pervasive imposter syndrome is, nothing will.

"The people you admire most are just as unsure of themselves as you are."

The problem with imposter syndrome isn't just the self-doubt—it's the way it holds you back. It whispers that you shouldn't apply for that promotion, speak up in that meeting, or take credit for your accomplishments. It convinces you that you're not ready, even when you are. And while humility has its place, imposter syndrome is not humility. It's self-sabotage.

But where does it come from? Part of the answer lies in perfectionism. Perfectionists often set impossibly high standards for themselves and feel like failures when they don't meet them. A 2018 study published in *Personality and Social Psychology Bulletin* found a strong link between perfectionism and imposter syndrome. The more you strive for flawlessness, the more you feel like a fraud when you inevitably fall short.

Another factor is comparison. Social media, for all its conveniences, has created a culture of constant comparison. Every day, you're bombarded with curated snapshots of other people's lives—their promotions, their vacations, their successes. What you don't see are their struggles, insecurities, and failures. As a result, you compare your unfiltered reality to everyone else's highlight reel, and you come up short.

Imposter syndrome is also fueled by systemic issues. Women and minorities, in particular, are more likely to experience it due to societal biases and stereotypes. When you're constantly told, explicitly or implicitly, that you don't belong, it's hard not to internalize that message. A 2021 study by *Harvard Business Review* found that women in male-dominated industries and people of color in predominantly white workplaces reported higher levels of imposter syndrome than their counterparts.

But here's the good news: imposter syndrome isn't permanent, and it isn't unbeatable. The first step to overcoming it is recognizing that it's normal. Feeling like an imposter doesn't mean you're unqualified—it means you care. It means you're stepping outside your comfort zone and challenging yourself. And that's where growth happens.

Take Howard Schultz, the former CEO of Starbucks. Schultz grew up in a housing complex for low-income families, and when he first entered the corporate world, he often felt out of place. He once said, "I'd walk into these big corporate offices and think, 'What am I doing here? They're going to figure out I don't belong.'" But instead of letting that fear paralyze him, Schultz used it as motivation. He leaned into his insecurities and built a company that redefined the coffee industry.

Another way to combat imposter syndrome is to focus on the facts. Imposter syndrome thrives on emotion, not evidence. When that voice in your head says, *You're not good enough,* ask yourself: What's the evidence for that? Chances are, you'll find more proof of your competence than your incompetence. Keep a record of your achievements—big or small—and revisit it when self-doubt creeps in.

"No matter how successful you get, no matter how accomplished, every once in a while you'll feel like a fraud."

— Michelle Obama

It's also important to talk about it. Imposter syndrome loves silence. It convinces you that you're the only one who feels this way, which makes the feeling even more isolating. But the moment you share your doubts with someone else, you'll realize how common they are. Talking to a mentor, colleague, or friend can help you gain perspective and see yourself through their eyes.

In 2018, Michelle Obama opened up about her own struggles with imposter syndrome. Despite her success as an attorney, First Lady, and global icon, she admitted to often feeling like she wasn't good enough. Her vulnerability resonated with millions and sparked a broader conversation about how self-doubt affects even the most accomplished individuals.

Finally, remember this: no one has it all figured out. Not your boss, not your mentor, not the person whose life looks perfect on Instagram. Everyone is winging it to some degree. The next time you feel like an imposter, remind yourself that the people you admire probably feel the same way. The difference is that they keep going anyway.

Imposter syndrome might never go away entirely, but it doesn't have to control you. Every time you push through it, every time you show up despite your doubts, you're proving it wrong. And with each step forward, you're rewriting the narrative. You're not an imposter. You're a work in progress—and that's more than enough.

Chapter 18:

Lessons from the Legends: Failing on a Billionaire Budget

Failure is often viewed as a stepping stone for the ambitious and the determined. But what happens when failure occurs on a scale so massive, so public, that it seems impossible to recover from? When the stakes are billions of dollars, entire industries, or reputations that span decades? Even at the top, failure is an equal-opportunity disruptor. The difference lies in how legends handle it, what they learn, and how they pivot to come back stronger.

Take Richard Branson, founder of the Virgin Group. Branson's entrepreneurial career is filled with high-profile failures, each more dramatic than the last. Virgin Cola, launched in 1994, was his attempt to take on giants like Coca-Cola and Pepsi. He boldly predicted that Virgin Cola would dominate the market within a year. Instead, it was an unmitigated disaster. The product flopped, retailers stopped stocking it, and Virgin Cola became a textbook example of overconfidence in business. Branson didn't shy away from admitting the failure. In his autobiography, he called it "one of the most expensive mistakes of my life." But instead of letting Virgin Cola define his career, Branson moved on, channeling his energy into ventures like Virgin Atlantic and Virgin Galactic. He embraced failure as an integral part of the process, famously saying, "Business opportunities are like buses; there's always another one coming."

The Branson story highlights a critical lesson about failure: diversification. Legends don't put all their eggs in one basket. They take calculated risks, knowing that not every venture will succeed. This approach minimizes the damage of individual failures while keeping the door open for future opportunities.

"Even billionaires blow it—the difference is they never stop moving forward."

Another billionaire who has mastered the art of failing forward is Elon Musk. Musk's ventures have revolutionized industries, but they've also teetered on the edge of disaster more times than most entrepreneurs would care to admit. In 2008, Tesla was on the brink of bankruptcy, and SpaceX had burned through its first three rocket launches without a single success. Musk himself admitted, "There was a better-than-even chance that we would never get anything to orbit." The stakes were astronomical, but Musk didn't give up. The fourth SpaceX launch succeeded, securing a crucial NASA contract, and Tesla narrowly avoided collapse thanks to a last-minute investment deal. Musk's ability to endure public failure, learn from it, and persevere is a defining characteristic of his success.

Musk's story underscores another key lesson: resilience. Failure isn't a death sentence; it's data. Each rocket explosion taught SpaceX engineers what to fix. Each missed delivery target taught Tesla how to optimize production. By treating failure as an opportunity for iteration rather than an endpoint, Musk turned near-catastrophes into stepping stones for innovation.

But failure isn't just about the big, dramatic moments—it's about the quiet, personal struggles that come with leadership. Indra Nooyi, the former CEO of PepsiCo, faced significant pushback when she shifted the company's focus toward healthier products. Critics argued that she was abandoning PepsiCo's core identity, and early sales numbers seemed to confirm their fears. Nooyi's decision to prioritize long-term sustainability over short-term profits wasn't an easy sell, and she faced intense scrutiny from shareholders. Yet, she stood by her vision, investing in research, marketing, and new product lines. By the time she stepped down in 2018, PepsiCo had not only diversified its portfolio but also increased revenue by more than 80% during her tenure.

Nooyi's journey highlights a different kind of failure: the failure to be universally understood or appreciated in the moment. Her story demonstrates the importance of conviction and long-term thinking. Sometimes, the path to success means weathering criticism and staying the course, even when the results aren't immediately visible.

And then there's the tale of Sam Walton, the founder of Walmart. In the early days of his retail career, Walton was forced to close his first store after his landlord refused to renew the lease. It was a crushing blow—one that could have ended his entrepreneurial dreams. Instead, Walton used the experience as a learning opportunity, identifying what worked and what didn't in his first venture. Armed with that knowledge, he went on to create Walmart, which grew into the largest retailer in the world. Walton often credited his early failure with teaching him the value of resilience, adaptability, and humility.

Failure doesn't just teach practical lessons; it reshapes character. A 2020 study published in the *Academy of Management Journal* found that leaders who experienced significant failures early in their careers were more likely to demonstrate empathy, humility, and emotional intelligence later in life. These traits, in turn, made them more effective at building trust and leading teams.

"I have not failed. I've just found 10,000 ways that won't work."

— Thomas Edison

Consider Oprah Winfrey, who was fired from her first television job in Baltimore for being "unfit for TV." The rejection could have ended her broadcasting career before it began. Instead, Oprah used it as motivation to carve out a space where she could be authentic. That space eventually became *The Oprah Winfrey Show*, a cultural phenomenon that redefined daytime television. Oprah's willingness to embrace her uniqueness, even after being told it was a liability, transformed her greatest perceived weakness into her most significant strength.

What unites these stories is not just the scale of the failures but the mindset behind the comebacks. Legends see failure as an inevitable part of the journey, not an aberration. They expect it, prepare for it, and use it to their advantage. They don't let their egos get in the way of learning. They don't let setbacks stop them from moving forward. And perhaps most importantly, they don't confuse failure with finality.

For every Branson, Musk, Nooyi, Walton, or Winfrey, there are countless others who didn't make it, who let failure define them instead of learning from it. The difference isn't talent or luck—it's mindset. Failure doesn't pick favorites, but how you respond to it can make or break your story.

So what can you take away from the legends? First, expect to fail. It's not a matter of if; it's a matter of when. Second, treat every failure as a data point, a lesson, and a stepping stone. Third, remember that resilience, adaptability, and long-term vision are your greatest tools. And finally, never stop moving forward. Because the legends didn't succeed despite their failures—they succeeded because of them.

Chapter 19:

Risking It All: When to Go All In (And When Not To)

Risk is often romanticized. The daring leap, the all-or-nothing gamble, the moment when someone bets everything on an idea, a dream, or a vision of a better future. It's the stuff of movies and motivational speeches. But in real life, taking big risks isn't just about courage—it's about calculation. The line between a bold move and a reckless one is thin, and knowing when to go all in—and when to hold back—can make all the difference.

The truth is, not all risks are created equal. Some are strategic and measured, while others are impulsive and dangerous. The difference isn't just in the outcome but in how the risk is approached. Take Jeff Bezos, for example. When Bezos left his high-paying job at a hedge fund to start Amazon, it wasn't a spur-of-the-moment decision. He spent months researching the nascent internet retail market, creating a business plan, and weighing the pros and cons. Bezos even developed what he called a "regret minimization framework," asking himself whether he would regret not taking the leap when he was 80 years old. The answer was yes, so he went all in—but not without a plan.

The concept of calculated risk isn't new, but it's often overlooked in a culture that glorifies fearless ambition. A 2019 study published in *Harvard Business Review* analyzed over 1,000 entrepreneurs and found that those who took calculated risks—carefully weighing potential rewards against possible downsides—were significantly more likely to succeed than those who acted impulsively. The lesson? Courage is essential, but so is preparation.

But what happens when the stakes are so high that failure isn't just a possibility—it's likely? That's where the stories of people like Chesley "Sully" Sullenberger come in. In 2009, Captain Sullenberger famously landed US Airways Flight 1549 on the Hudson River after both engines failed. The successful water landing, which saved all 155 passengers and crew onboard, was hailed as a miracle. But it wasn't luck. Sullenberger's decision to ditch the plane in the Hudson wasn't an impulsive gamble; it was the result of years of training, experience, and composure under pressure. He knew the risks, assessed his options, and acted decisively. His story is a testament to the power of preparation in high-stakes situations.

"Knowing when to walk away is just as bold as knowing when to leap."

Sometimes, going all in isn't about a single moment—it's about sustained risk over time. Consider Malala Yousafzai, who became an international symbol of courage after being shot by the Taliban for advocating girls' education. Malala's decision to speak out wasn't made lightly. She and her family understood the risks but believed the cause was worth it. After surviving the attack, Malala didn't retreat; she doubled down, using her platform to campaign for global education initiatives. Her story is a reminder that the most meaningful risks are often the ones with no guaranteed reward.

But not every risk is worth taking. Sometimes, the smartest move is knowing when to say no. In 2001, Mark Cuban, the billionaire entrepreneur, was offered the chance to invest in the airline industry. Despite the potential for high returns, Cuban declined, citing the industry's volatility and slim profit margins. His decision proved wise when the events of September 11th sent the airline industry into a tailspin. Cuban's story illustrates an important point: sometimes, the boldest move is walking away.

Another example of knowing when to hold back comes from the world of sports. Serena Williams, one of the greatest tennis players of all time, has consistently demonstrated an ability to balance risk and restraint. In 2017, Williams won the Australian Open while pregnant—a feat that required calculated decisions about how far to push her body. After giving birth, she faced complications that forced her to step back and prioritize her health. Williams' willingness to weigh risks and make difficult choices has been instrumental in her longevity and success.

So how do you decide when to go all in and when to pull back? The first step is understanding your risk tolerance. A 2020 study in the *Journal of Behavioral Economics* found that people's willingness to take risks is influenced by their personality, experiences, and circumstances. Risk tolerance isn't a fixed trait; it changes over time and varies depending on the context. Recognizing your own comfort level with uncertainty can help you make better decisions.

The second step is asking the right questions. What's the best-case scenario? What's the worst-case scenario? Can you live with the downside? What will you lose if you don't take the risk? These questions force you to confront the reality of the situation, rather than getting swept up in emotion or overconfidence.

"Fortune favors the brave."

— Latin Proverb

And finally, you have to embrace the possibility of failure. Risk, by definition, involves uncertainty. Even the most calculated moves can go sideways. In 2016, Kobe Bryant retired from basketball after a 20-year career with the Los Angeles Lakers. Bryant didn't stop taking risks; he shifted his focus to storytelling, founding Granity Studios and producing content that reflected his passion for creativity. His animated short film *Dear Basketball* won an Academy Award in 2018, proving that success in a new arena often requires the same willingness to risk failure.

But not every risk pays off. Elon Musk, for all his successes, has faced significant failures, including the near-collapse of Tesla and SpaceX. Oprah Winfrey's early television career was marked by rejections. Steve Jobs was famously ousted from Apple before making a legendary return. The common thread in all these stories isn't the absence of failure—it's the persistence to try again.

The truth about risk is that it's never one-and-done. Life is a series of calculated bets, some of which pay off and some of which don't. The key is learning from the losses, adapting, and knowing when to go all in—and when to walk away. Because in the end, success isn't about avoiding risk; it's about managing it. It's about taking the leap, even when you're not sure where you'll land. And it's about trusting yourself to figure it out, no matter what happens next.

Common Outcomes of Failure

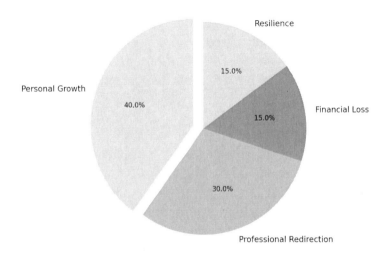

Common Outcomes of Failure

This chart highlights the typical results of failure. While financial loss and setbacks occur, the majority of outcomes—such as personal growth, professional redirection, and resilience—underscore the transformative power of failure.

Chapter 20:

Your Fearless Finish: Writing Your Own Comeback Story

Failure is inevitable, but what happens after it is entirely up to you. It can be the weight that crushes you or the force that propels you forward. The choice is yours, and the process is simple, though never easy: you write your own comeback story. Not by erasing the failures, but by building on them. Not by pretending they didn't happen, but by proving that they didn't define you.

Comebacks aren't exclusive to underdog sports movies or redemption arcs in Hollywood. They're real, raw, and messy, and they happen every day in the lives of ordinary people. Whether it's a career derailed, a relationship shattered, or a dream seemingly out of reach, comebacks start with one critical decision: the choice to try again.

Think about Howard Schultz's return to Starbucks in 2008. Schultz had stepped away as CEO years earlier, and the company lost its focus, chasing rapid growth at the expense of quality. Starbucks was in decline, with its stock plummeting and its stores losing the charm that had made them so popular. Schultz could have walked away, but instead, he chose to return and reclaim the company's soul. His comeback wasn't instant, nor was it easy. He closed over 600 underperforming stores, retrained baristas, and doubled down on Starbucks' original mission. By the time he stepped down again in 2017, Starbucks was thriving. Schultz's comeback wasn't just about saving a company—it was about proving that course correction is always possible.

Comebacks often require a willingness to step into discomfort. In 2016, Simone Biles walked away from the gymnastics spotlight after winning four gold medals at the Rio Olympics. The pressure to stay on top was immense, but Biles chose to focus on her mental health and personal growth. When she returned to competition years later, she did so on her terms, prioritizing her well-being while still demonstrating her incredible talent. Her story is a reminder that comebacks aren't about returning to the status quo—they're about redefining success in a way that aligns with who you are.

"Failure is just the setup for your greatest success."

For others, a comeback means finding new purpose after devastating loss. In 1993, Michael Jordan shocked the world by retiring from basketball following the murder of his father. At the height of his career, Jordan walked away from the sport that had defined him. He spent the next two years pursuing baseball, honoring a dream his father had held for him. While his baseball career was far from stellar, it gave Jordan the space to grieve and rediscover his passion for basketball. When he returned to the NBA in 1995, he didn't just pick up where he left off—he led the Chicago Bulls to three consecutive championships, cementing his legacy as one of the greatest athletes of all time. Jordan's comeback wasn't about proving others wrong; it was about finding his way back to himself.

But comebacks aren't limited to individuals. Organizations, too, can rise from the ashes of failure. Take Ford Motor Company in the early 2000s. The iconic automaker was losing billions of dollars annually, its reputation battered by outdated designs and declining quality. In 2006, Ford hired Alan Mulally as CEO, and his turnaround strategy became a masterclass in resilience. Mulally refocused the company on its core values, streamlined operations, and secured a massive loan to avoid bankruptcy—unlike its competitors, General Motors and Chrysler, which required government bailouts. By the time Mulally retired in 2014, Ford had not only returned to profitability but also reclaimed its place as a leader in the auto industry. Ford's comeback wasn't about reinventing the wheel; it was about remembering what had made it great in the first place.

Comebacks are rarely linear. They're filled with setbacks, false starts, and moments of doubt. In 2014, Cheryl Strayed, author of *Wild*, reflected on her journey from rock bottom to best-selling author. In her twenties, Strayed's life was in shambles—her mother had died, her marriage had ended, and she was struggling with addiction. Determined to find herself, she embarked on a 1,100-mile solo hike along the Pacific Crest Trail. That journey became the foundation for her memoir, which resonated with millions and was later adapted into a film starring Reese Witherspoon. Strayed's story isn't just about the hike; it's about her decision to turn her pain into something meaningful.

What all these stories have in common is a refusal to let failure have the last word. Comebacks aren't about erasing mistakes—they're about building on them. They're about taking the lessons learned and using them as stepping stones to something greater.

"It always seems impossible until it's done."

— Nelson Mandela

A 2021 study published in *Psychological Science* found that people who viewed their failures as opportunities for growth were significantly more likely to achieve long-term success than those who internalized their failures as personal flaws. The study underscores a crucial point: your mindset matters. How you frame your failures shapes how you approach your comeback.

It's easy to get stuck in the narrative of defeat. The missed opportunities, the wrong turns, the "what ifs" that play on a loop in your mind. But the truth is, those moments don't define you unless you let them. Every great comeback starts with a choice: to stop replaying the past and start rewriting the future.

When Walt Disney's first animation company went bankrupt, he didn't let it stop him. He used the failure to refine his craft, eventually creating the most beloved entertainment empire in history. When Nelson Mandela spent 27 years in prison, he didn't let it break him. He emerged with a vision of reconciliation that transformed a nation. When Vera Wang failed to make the U.S. Olympic figure skating team, she didn't give up—she pivoted, building a career in fashion that made her an icon.

Your comeback doesn't have to be as grand as these examples. It might be about rebuilding a career after losing a job, mending a relationship after a falling out, or rediscovering your passion after years of neglect. What matters isn't the scale of the comeback—it's the commitment to start again.

So how do you write your own comeback story? Start with a decision. Decide that your failures are not the end of the road but the beginning of a new chapter. Reflect on what went wrong, but don't dwell there. Use the lessons you've learned to guide your next steps. Surround yourself with people who believe in your potential, even when you doubt it yourself. And most importantly, take action. Even the smallest steps can build momentum.

Comebacks aren't about perfection—they're about progress. They're about showing up, even when it's hard, and trusting that every effort brings you closer to the life you want. Because the truth is, failure isn't final. It's just the setup for the fearless finish you're about to write.

Conclusion:

Fail Harder, Rise Stronger

Here's the truth: failure is inevitable. You're going to mess up, fall short, and face setbacks. You're going to have moments where nothing works out the way you planned, where everything feels like it's crumbling, and where you're convinced you've reached the end of the road. But here's the twist—failure isn't the end. It's the beginning.

Throughout this book, we've explored the messy, uncomfortable, and often painful reality of failure. From personal faceplants to billion-dollar blowups, failure happens at every level. It happens to dreamers, doers, leaders, and legends. The difference isn't in whether you fail—it's in how you respond.

Do you let failure define you? Do you let it paralyze you? Or do you use it as a springboard to come back stronger? The choice is always yours.

By now, you know that failure isn't just something to survive—it's something to embrace. It's the world's most honest teacher, stripping away ego and pretense to show you exactly where you need to grow. It's the necessary friction that sparks innovation, creativity, and resilience. It's the thing that forces you to get real with yourself, to step up, and to keep going when the odds aren't in your favor.

Let's be clear: this isn't about romanticizing failure. It's not about seeking it out or pretending it doesn't hurt. Failure is hard. It's uncomfortable. It's messy. But it's also the birthplace of growth, the forge where your grit is tested and your character is built.

Take a moment to reflect on where you've been. Think about the times you've failed—the risks that didn't pay off, the relationships that fell apart, the dreams that didn't materialize. Now think about what those failures taught you. Maybe they showed you what you're capable of enduring. Maybe they forced you to change direction. Maybe they prepared you for something you didn't even know was coming. Whatever they did, they didn't stop you. You're still here.

And if you're still here, you've got everything you need to write your comeback story.

Failure isn't about the fall—it's about the rise. It's about learning from the lessons, adapting to the challenges, and refusing to let setbacks have the final say. It's about stepping back into the arena, even when you're bruised and battered, because you know that nothing worth having comes easy.

As you turn the final page of this book, I hope you walk away with a new perspective on failure. I hope you see it not as something to fear but as something to face head-on. I hope you take bigger risks, aim higher, and fail harder—not because failure is the goal, but because it's the only way to grow.

The world doesn't need more people playing it safe. It needs people willing to try, willing to fail, and willing to keep going. It needs people like you.

So go out there and take the leap. Mess up, learn, adapt, and try again. And when you fail—and you will—remember this: failure isn't a reflection of your worth. It's proof that you're trying, that you're daring, that you're alive. It's the bridge between who you are and who you're becoming.

Fail harder. Rise stronger. Keep going. Your story isn't over yet.

Specific References by Chapter Themes

Chapter 2: The Comfort Zone

6. Pink, Daniel H. *Drive: The Surprising Truth About What Motivates Us*. Riverhead Books, 2011.
   - Explores the dangers of comfort and the role of intrinsic motivation.
7. Collins, Jim. *Good to Great: Why Some Companies Make the Leap and Others Don't*. HarperBusiness, 2001.
   - Discusses the transformative power of stepping out of comfort zones.

Chapter 3: Fail Fast, Fail Loud, Fail Proud

8. Gelles, David. *"How to Be Resilient." The New York Times*, 2017.
   - Offers practical strategies for learning from failure quickly.
9. Ries, Eric. *The Lean Startup: How Today's Entrepreneurs Use Continuous Innovation to Create Radically Successful Businesses*. Crown Business, 2011.
   - Promotes a "fail fast" approach for iterative improvement.

Chapter 7: The Science of Screwing Up

10. American Psychological Association. *"Building Your Resilience."*
    - Highlights the science behind bouncing back from failure.
11. Jordan, Matthew. *"Why Failure Drives Innovation." Forbes*, 2018.

- Explains how failure enhances problem-solving and creativity.

Chapter 10: Turning a Faceplant Into a Launchpad

12. Rowling, J.K. *"The Fringe Benefits of Failure."* Harvard Commencement Speech, 2008.
- Personal reflections on how failure paved the way for success.
13. Robinson, Ken. *"Do Schools Kill Creativity?"* TED Talk.
- Discusses the role of failure in fostering creativity and innovation.

Chapter 15: Fail Harder, Love Smarter

14. Brown, Brené. *The Gifts of Imperfection: Let Go of Who You Think You're Supposed to Be and Embrace Who You Are.* Hazelden Publishing, 2010.
- Explores vulnerability and connection in relationships.

Industry-Specific Failures and Lessons

Space Exploration (Chapter 4, Chapter 18)

15. Davenport, Christian. *The Space Barons: Elon Musk, Jeff Bezos, and the Quest to Colonize the Cosmos.* PublicAffairs, 2018.
- Chronicles the failures and breakthroughs of SpaceX and Blue Origin.

Technology (Chapters 4, 18)

16. Isaacson, Walter. *Steve Jobs.* Simon & Schuster, 2011.
- Highlights the failures and resilience behind Apple's innovation.

Healthcare (Chapter 18)

17. Parker, Clifton B. *"Failure as the Key to Innovation." Stanford Business Insights,* 2014.
- Discusses the role of failure in groundbreaking medical advancements.

Psychological and Emotional References

Imposter Syndrome (Chapter 17)

18. Clance, Pauline R., and Suzanne A. Imes. *"The Imposter Phenomenon in High Achieving Women: Dynamics and Therapeutic Intervention." Psychotherapy: Theory, Research & Practice,* vol. 15, no. 3, 1978, pp. 241–247.

Burnout Recovery (Chapter 16)

19. Lamott, Anne. *Bird by Bird: Some Instructions on Writing and Life.* Anchor, 1994.
- Insights on creativity, resilience, and starting again.

The Emotional Cycle of Failure (Chapter 6)

20. Kubler-Ross, Elisabeth. *On Grief and Grieving: Finding the Meaning of Grief Through the Five Stages of Loss.* Scribner, 2005.
- A foundational text on processing emotions during difficult transitions.

Cultural and Historical Figures

21. Mandela, Nelson. *Long Walk to Freedom: The Autobiography of Nelson Mandela.* Little, Brown and Company, 1994.
22. Branson, Richard. *Losing My Virginity: How I Survived, Had Fun, and Made a Fortune Doing Business My Way.* Crown Business, 2011.
23. Angelou, Maya. *I Know Why the Caged Bird Sings.* Random House, 1969.
- Maya Angelou's reflections on overcoming personal struggles.

Additional Resources

Research on Risk-Taking (Chapter 19)

24. Gallup. *"The Global State of Risk-Taking in Business."*
25. Harvard Business Review. *"The Right Way to Take Risks."*

Index